VIETNAM FIRE MISSION

For my family and friends

Cover photo: Corporal Larry Hilton, with the 1st 155mm Gun Battery, USMC at Phu Bai, Vietnam in 1967. This massive weapon is an "155mm Gun, Self Propelled, M53." He is also holding an M-14 rifle with a "40" round magazine, which he made in Vietnam.

VIETNAM FIRE MISSION

FIGHTING WITH THE 1ST 155MM GUN BATTERY (SELF-PROPELLED), USMC

LARRY ALLEN HILTON

Pen & Sword
MILITARY

AN IMPRINT OF PEN & SWORD BOOKS LTD.
YORKSHIRE – PHILADELPHIA

First published in Great Britain in 2025 by
PEN AND SWORD MILITARY
An imprint of
Pen & Sword Books Ltd
Yorkshire – Philadelphia

ISBN 978 1 03611 423 7

Typeset by SJmagic DESIGN SERVICES, India.

Printed and bound in the UK by CPI Group (UK) Ltd.

The Publisher's authorised representative in the EU for product safety is
Authorised Rep Compliance Ltd., Ground Floor, 71 Lower Baggot Street, Dublin
D02 P593, Ireland. www.arccompliance.com

For a complete list of Pen & Sword titles please contact
PEN & SWORD BOOKS LIMITED
George House, Units 12 & 13, Beevor Street, Off Pontefract Road,
Barnsley, South Yorkshire, S71 1HN, England
E-mail: enquiries@pen-and-sword.co.uk
Website: www.pen-and-sword.co.uk

or

PEN AND SWORD BOOKS
1950 Lawrence Rd, Havertown, PA 19083, USA
E-mail: uspen-and-sword@casematepublishers.com
Website: www.penandswordbooks.com

FSC
www.fsc.org
MIX
Paper | Supporting
responsible forestry
FSC® C013604

Contents

Foreword

"Fire Mission…
…Battery Adjust;
Gun 6, one round…
… Shell HE;
Full Charge;
Fuze Point Detonating (PD)……
Deflection 2654;
Quadrant 623……
8 Rounds in effect."
"Stand by–"
"FIRE!"

These are the words we would describe today as the fire commands normally given to a Marine artillery Section Chief. The "Chief" was the Marine NCO in charge of the gun or howitzer section (or crew), and their weapon – a 105mm, 155mm or 8-inch howitzer, or the unique M53 self-propelled 155mm gun. The section loaded, aimed, and fired the 35–200 pound projectiles employed with these weapons safely and accurately. The specific intent was to cause the physical destruction and maximum casualties to an enemy force.

"The mission of the field artillery (FA) is to destroy, neutralize, or suppress the enemy by cannon, rocket, and missile fires…"

While technology and the specific artillery howitzers and gun models employed have changed over time in the Marine Corps, the fire commands set out above have changed little since World War Two. The prescribed personnel requirement for a gun section for manning and operating an

M53 155mm gun or an M55 8-inch howitzer was twelve Marines and one section chief. The Section Chief in peacetime was "normally" required to be an experienced, seasoned Non-Commissioned Officer (NCO) with six to eight years' time in service.

Unfortunately, in the early years of the Vietnam War, Marine artillery sections were "normally" under-manned, and "normally" led by very young and very junior Marines with only one to two years' time in service. Such was the experience of one young Marine Lance Corporal named Larry Hilton, who served his country in Vietnam for thirteen months in 1966–7.

This book is Larry Hilton's story. It's an important story that needs to be told. There are many books written about the Vietnam War from the perspective of an infantryman or pilot … but very few written by an artilleryman. An artilleryman is a "different animal," with a different job, different responsibilities, and at times, facing different dangers. As he was told by a senior NCO following boot camp, "Don't worry, as an artilleryman in Vietnam, you will have plenty of opportunities to go on patrol in the jungle with only your rifle, extra ammunition and a few hand grenades." These words would in fact turn out to be very true.

This is the memoir of a young man from humble beginnings, who grew up in Southern California. Filled with thoughts of adventure … and a sense of responsibility to "fight and serve" his country, Larry enlisted in the Marine Corps upon graduating from high school. Following Marine Corps Recruit Training and a short first stop in Camp Lejeune, North Carolina, he found himself in Vietnam, assigned to the 1st 155mm Gun Battery (Self-Propelled) in I Corps. Through a very short period, Larry served at first as a basic cannoneer, as the gun's loader and as a "powder monkey" running back and forth from an ammunition pile to keep his cannon fed. This was followed by assignment to assistant gunner, then gunner, and finally, at 20 years of age, Lance Corporal Hilton was assigned duties as Section Chief of Gun number 6 – a 155mm Gun, Self-Propelled M53. Once appointed to this new responsibility Larry discovered that instead of having a twelve- to thirteen-man gun section, young Lance Corporal Hilton had only five or six junior Marines to crew his gun.

This book describes Larry's thirteen months in Vietnam, where his section fired countless artillery fire missions, patrolled in the jungle like any other Marine unit and manned the wire perimeters and listening posts at night. Larry and his section endured enemy mortar attacks and dealt with the random rifle fire from Viet Cong and NVA snipers. This true story is filled with the fear, humor, sadness, camaraderie, exhaustion, loneliness, and horror of war. We also find the spirituality and willingness to make-do in tough circumstances which typifies the young Marine serving in combat.

The Vietnam War and Larry's experience as a Marine artilleryman have always remained with him. Unfortunately, the insidious effects of Agent Orange will eventually take a physical toll on him and his family, and Larry then joins the ranks of the thousands of disabled Vietnam veterans living in America. Through his faith in God and the support of a loving wife and family, Larry remains proud of his Marine Corps service and the sacrifices he made while serving his country. This is his story.

David J. Barile
Colonel, USMC (Retired)
Marine Artilleryman

Acknowledgements

First and foremost, I want to thank the Lord for His faithfulness throughout my life. I didn't always see it, but I know He was and is watching over me.

To the many who have encouraged me to put these stories into a book over the past several years, I cannot thank you enough. This book probably would not have happened if it were not for you.

I want to thank my wife and family for listening to these stories over and over.

Kasey, our youngest daughter, started me out with a blog and editing stories several years ago. She would say, "Post that story on Facebook. It needs to be seen and read." This book would never have been written without her help.

MP Robinson, a Canadian historian with an enduring interest in Marine Corps operations throughout the Vietnam War, edited my original drafts and helped me though the process of finding a publisher. We first made contact while he was researching his book "American Artillery in Vietnam", which explains the missions of the thousands of US Army and USMC cannoneers and cannon cockers throughout that war. He lives in Canada in the Toronto area with his wife and children, and he has published over a dozen military books since 2015.

Preface

Every Marine is a rifleman, but not every Marine is an infantryman. There are over one hundred Military Occupational Specialties (MOS) in the US Marine Corps. I did not know this when I enlisted at 18 years old. I thought everyone in the Marines was an infantryman. I did not know they had cooks, clerks, and cannoneers. The MOS for artillery is 0811, cannoneer, or cannon cocker as they are called in the Marines.

Now, I had joined the Marines to carry a rifle and to be in the infantry. On my last day of boot camp, I was told I was to be an artilleryman – what we Marines called a cannon cocker. Now people may say the artillery is behind the lines, that artillery was a safe place to be. Maybe in World War Two and Korea it was a safe place to be, but not in Vietnam. In Victnam there were no front lines, and no safe places to be. Often in Vietnam a battery of artillery was set up by all themselves in the middle of nowhere.

Somebody once asked me, "Why would a Marine in the artillery need a rifle"? Well, batteries were prestigious targets in Vietnam. Artillery batteries hit their targets and do an untold amount of damage to an enemy, even one like the VC or NVA. Our batteries were regularly attacked by snipers, 60mm and 82mm mortars, specially trained enemy sappers, VC guerillas and NVA regulars on an almost constant basis. Eventually, the mortar attacks become 122mm and 140mm rocket attacks. We had to defend ourselves.

By the time I went to Vietnam the Marines had already been there for more than a year. The 3rd Marine Division on Okinawa got the call to deploy to Vietnam in March 1965. Somebody said, "We are going to war." "What war?", another marine asked. "Vietnam" – which begged the question "Where's Vietnam?". Many Americans had no idea was before March 1965.

That was not an uncommon conversation among the Marines in the spring of 1965. Having met and talked to many Marines who had made the landings in Da Nang in March 1965, it was pretty plain to see that men had been pulled from Marine postings all over the Pacific in order to get the number of men necessary to deploy. Some guys told me that Marine units were in the field training in Okinawa and Japan on one day and then shipping out the next. One Marine said he was in a supply unit when the landings took place, and that he was told to find a ride to Vietnam. When he arrived, he was put into an infantry unit and handed a 3.5inch rocket launcher. Those rocket launchers were designed to blow up tanks. He thought it was kind of funny walking around in the rice paddies carrying that thing. Another Marine told me he was in Japan and was told to go to Vietnam. He said he didn't have his rifle, gear, or sea-bag. He was told that his rifle and gear would catch up with him in Vietnam. In March of 1965 any Marines whose term of service was expected to end shortly were informed that their service in the Marine Corps had been extended by four months. This created a great many very angry Marines, and I met several of them.

I should also mention the "fog of war." It was sometimes hard for back then to remember the exact names, dates, and places where things happened. I will give an example. Throughout my whole life since leaving the Marine Corps I could not remember where I was 10 November 1966. 10 November is the US Marines Corps' birthday, and it is celebrated. That date is something every marine would remember. I know for certain that I was in Vietnam, but why couldn't I remember that day? I'd say it was the fog of war.

The mystery was solved almost fifty years later when Bob Simington, a Marine from the 1st Guns' Fire Direction Center (FDC) sent me a picture in 2015 asking me, "Is this you?" Yes, it was me in Vietnam on 10 November 1966. In the photo I'm standing in the color guard for the ceremony at the mess hall in Phu Bai waiting for the cake. That shows that under the stressful conditions of a war zone, sometimes memory fails. And so, to the best of my ability, I have recounted the story of my time in Vietnam as truthfully as I know how. When those Marines landed on the beaches of Da Nang, Vietnam, in March 1965, that was the start of a great adventure for me. I joined the Marine Corps and volunteered to go to Vietnam, and so my adventure began.

Larry Hilton

Chapter 1

Growing Up in Southern California

My parents had been farmers in Arizona before World War Two, but they moved to Los Angeles, California, in 1941. They wanted a better life than living on a farm in Arizona. Somebody went and stole their car the first day they arrived in LA – welcome to Sunny Southern California! My father found work as a machinist and my mother became a beautician. I am the middle of three children. My oldest brother Ronald Hilton was

View of the San Gabriel Mountains in Southern California. 10,000ft high. (Courtesy Roy Funk)

Mike Varley and me 1953.

born on 3 June 1944. I was born on 12 December 1946, and my youngest brother LeRoy Hilton was born on 23 April 1953. We lived in Maywood, California, until we moved to West Covina, California, on 25 December 1953. I remember that Christmas Day well: we opened a few gifts that morning and then headed to our new home.

From our new home in West Covina we could see the whole panorama of beautiful landscapes. We could see mountains rising from 5,000 to 10,000ft high to the north of our house. It was beautiful. There were orange groves everywhere. There were lots of fruit trees and flowers because Southern California has a 300-day growing season. In those beautiful surroundings I made some good friends. I met Mike Varley in 1953 and Roy Bell in 1954. We were just 6, 7 and 8 years old. If you saw one of us, you usually saw all three of us. They enjoyed adventures outdoors just like me. We hiked, biked, slept over at each other's houses as often as we could, and sometimes even camped outside. Later, as teenagers, we learned to drive and we started taking our adventures all over Southern California and beyond.

Above left: Me, 8 years old. Cub Scout.

Above right: Mike Varley and Roy Bell as teenagers. (Courtesy Michael Varley)

We all joined the Cub Scouts. My dad was the treasurer of the group and other parents were involved too. Many of the moms were Den Mothers. It was fun, and we had some great times and memories. I stayed in the Cub Scouts until I made the grade of Webelos, which is the second highest rank before going into the Boy Scouts. I never joined the Boy Scouts, but it was a very good organization.

When it snowed in the mountains our parents took several of us up there to experience it. I do not ever remember it snowing in the West Covina area. The mountains were just beautiful after it had snowed. There were many other times in warmer weather when we went to the beach for the day.

Living in Southern California in the 1950s and 60s was a fantastic adventure. We hung around the many construction sites as the orange groves were being bulldozed over, and houses, schools, and shopping centers were being built. I spent many days in the orange groves, hiking up into the hills, and bicycling all over Covina and West Covina. My friends and I spent a lot of time at the beaches surfing as we got older, or going into the desert looking for, and finding, old cars. We were especially keen on Model A Fords but we'd take an interest in just about any cars that people had been dumping in the desert since the 1940s to get rid of. It seemed that everything was within an hour's drive of West Covina.

The Hilton family (and friends) in the snow.

We visited our grandparents every summer on the farm in Arizona as a family. Our mom and dad wanted us to get on the farm and also to help our grandparents during those summer months. My brother Ron and I spent a few summers living on the farm. I recall arriving and digging a new latrine beside the old outhouse, then pulling the wooden two seat outhouse over to the new hole and finally shoveling the dirt into the old latrine to fill it in. The grim reality sunk in quickly that we were on a real farm, and there was plenty of hard work.

Ron and I milked a cow twice a day, hoed the vegetable garden, washed clothes in big buckets, and cut firewood for the wood-burning stove that my grandmother cooked on daily. We also killed chickens and geese for dinner, collected eggs from the chicken house, fed chickens and took care of a flock of sheep. We took our baths in a nearby stream. These labors were just some of the many things that filled our days on the farm.

I believe that all these many hours out of doors and on the farm prepared me for my thirteen months in Vietnam. I was an outdoor person and had slept outside with my friends frequently while growing up, when every day seemed to be an adventure for us. Our parents encouraged us to either play sports or find a part time job. There was little time to just sit around and that was fine by me. In the fifth and sixth grades I played several sports, but I also mowed lawns, sold Kool-Aid to workmen, and had a paper route. When I was in seventh grade my mom told me I had to start buying my own clothes. Fortunately, I wore T-shirts, 501 Levi's, and tennis shoes so it was not a big expense for me.

In 7th and 8th grade when I was 13 and 14 years old my interests started shifting. Go-karts, minibikes, and cars kept me busy and out of trouble, and they brought my dad and me closer together when I was in the 8th and 9th grade. Once when I was just 14 years old, my dad had to take the new 1960 Chevy to the gas station. He told me to follow him in the old

My youngest brother LeRoy and I are standing by the 1950 Chevrolet at the farm in Camp Verde, Arizona.

1950 Chevy that was a standard shift three on the column. I had never driven a car with a clutch before. He took off and headed to the gas station. I got in the old 1950 Chevy and backed out of the driveway into the street and took off after him. I guess he thought it was time for me to start driving.

My older brother Ron bought a 1930 Model "A" Ford two-door coupe, but the engine was frozen up because it had sat for such a long time. Night after night, Mike Varley and I would work on Ron's car. I remember taking the engine apart and putting it back together. What a great learning experience that turned out to be for me. Loud backfires could be heard from the garage as I was trying to get the engine started. Finally, my dad came out into the garage and told me I had the timing off. I still had no idea what "timing" even was! Dad opened a book and read something, then went over to the engine and said I was one position off "top dead center". He showed me how to make the corrections and then said, "Try it now". The old 1930 Model "A" Ford started right up. My Dad was smarter than I thought. The 1930 Ford was my older brother's car, but I worked on it and drove it a lot before he sold it for $150.

When I turned 16 years old and got my driver's license, I already knew how to drive. My father made an extra set of keys to his 1950 Chevy which

Above: Here's Melinda Anderson Simon, Jon Kennedy, and Dave Wilson by Jon's 1930 Model "A" Ford. (Courtesy of Melinda Anderson Simon)

Left: Rich Roberts had a 1929 Ford Model "A" Roadster. It had a Cadillac V8 engine in it. (Courtesy Rich Roberts)

he drove to work every day. When he came home from work that evening, I was standing in the driveway. He gave the keys to me and he said, "Drive across the country when you can. It's beautiful."

Eventually I bought a 1929 Model "A" Ford. Several of us young guys had old cars and would caravan around the streets of Covina. It was always a great time. You could find a Model "A" just about anywhere in California back in the 1960s.

While in High School in 1961, I worked about three hours each day after school at a bakery cleaning up after the bakers. Usually four hours on Saturdays. There were a ton of pots and pans to wash in that bakery. I was making 90 cents an hour and had more money than I knew what to do with. Gasoline was 19 to 20 cents a gallon when they had "gas wars", and a hamburger was 20 cents back in 1961.

I liked surfing, a popular sport in Southern California. I was just not very good at it. I had two surfboards, and almost drowned once. The Pacific Ocean had some big waves, and if you got caught underneath a set of those waves, it could be dangerous. I did have some nice rides and memories of the beach, but it all ended when a set of three big waves came up and I could not get on the outside of them.

The first wave took me backwards and I lost my surfboard. I was in deep water. I came to the top only to be hit and taken down by a second wave. I tried to go to the bottom and push myself to the top, but I could not find the bottom of the ocean floor. Finally, I came to the top and the third wave took me back to the bottom. I remember starting to cry under the water. The next thing I knew I was washed up on the beach, barely alive. I sold my two surfboards not long after that experience.

Chapter 2

America Was Going to War

On 8 March 1965, I was a senior in high school. While walking to my next class, I saw a bunch of guys standing in a big group. My first thought was that maybe there was a fight about to happen, or maybe a "Penny Stomp". That was where the boys formed a circle, and each would throw money into the middle. Anyone brave (or stupid) enough would try to pick up the money. But anyone so bold would often pay a heavy price of getting pounded by everyone else in the circle as they scrambled to pick up the money and would then be chased out of the circle.

My high school friend Allen Jagielo yelled to me from that group of guys that the US Marines had landed in Vietnam. My first thought was, "Vietnam was where that monk set himself on fire".

Everyone had seen that picture it seemed. Allen asked me if I was going to join the army and stop the communists, because he was planning to sign up to do just that. I thought that perhaps the military would be the next adventure for this Southern California boy. Then I wondered where Vietnam even was.

In my Senior year I had been working part-time in a machine shop that had a big government contract to finish off bomb parts. I only took and attended three classes in my senior year. I was told that I could graduate early if I wanted to, but I wanted to take a math class, a printing class, and a sex education class. I had already made plans to work full time in a machine shop after graduation, which I expected in June 1965. When I got to work at the machine shop at about noon each day, I went over to the railroad yard with a big truck and picked up thousands of pieces of bomb parts. The machinists had to cut them to a specific size. I found out later they were brass rings for the high explosive artillery rounds.

I was then making more money than I ever had before. I even brought home a paycheck and showed my father. I thought I would follow in his footsteps and be a machinist, until one day he asked me what I was planning to do with my life. "I'm going to be a machinist like you," was my answer.

He asked, "Do you really want to stand behind a machine all of your life?" That did seem kind of boring. My older brother Ron had moved out when he turned 18, which freed up lots of room for Leroy and I in our small bedroom (once we removed Ron's bed).

Ron had by then got a job with an airline, and he was traveling a great deal. He told me that life was different once you were out on your own, because you must buy toothpaste, toilet paper, and all the stuff that mom and dad always had always bought. This gave me cause to wonder if I too could make it on my own. Then in May 1965, Ron was drafted into the Army. He left for boot camp on 3 June, his 21st birthday. My parents got a call from him in Fort Polk, Louisiana, and he told them he was now in the United States Army. When I walked into the house that evening my mother and father seemed upset as they told me that Ron had been drafted.

In those days all of us boys had to sign up for the draft when we turned 18. There was an assembly at the high school for all the senior boys to listen to military recruiters speaking in the gymnasium. There were about 300 of us. Nobody was paying any attention until Gunnery Sergeant Miller,

Above left: My brother Ron, seen here home on leave after being drafted into the United States Army.

Above right: My Graduation June 1965, standing by my 1957 Chevy.

a Marine recruiter, stood up and walked over to the microphone. The dress blue uniform, his square jar, and hardly any hair, made quite the impression. Nobody said a word as he spoke a few words and ended by driving home his main point: "If you want to become a man, join the Marines." The Gunnery Sergeant then walked off the stage.

I graduated from Covina High School in June 1965. I went out and met the Marine recruiter Gunnery Sergeant Miller in his Azusa office in August. "Hello Lad," he said. "What can I help you with?" I told him I had been thinking about joining the Marines. I mentioned that I wanted to go to Vietnam. He tested me with a short written test. Gunny Miller had a program he held at his house where I could meet other guys going into the Marines. I would be starting boot camp on 9 September 1965.

It was at Gunny Miller's house that I met Bob Myers. He went to Northview High School. Bob and I became friends, and we were both planning to go into the Marines, but Bob would enter one year later. Two other friends from high school, Brad Begin and Don Caouette, joined when they found out I had signed up. They figured they would be getting the "GREETINGS" draft notice in the mail at any time. We joined together on the "Buddy System," which was supposed to mean we three would be in boot camp together. I always thought a normal enlistment in the Marines was four years, so believed we would serve the four years together. I was given a three-year enlistment, but Brad and Don both signed up for two-year enlistments.

What I did not know was that the marines had two- and three-year enlistments, plus a six-month service in the reserve. The reservist had to go through twelve weeks of boot camp, six months of active duty and then went to the city where they lived for meetings one weekend each month and two weeks in the summer for six years. But they could be called up to full time service if the Marine Corps activated the 4th Marine Division, which was the Marines' reserve division. Who would have known? What's more, we all did go into boot camp at San Diego, but we never saw each other even once again during basic training and we were all sent to different places once we were through the training. So much for the "Buddy System"!

Chapter 3

Marine Corps Recruit Depot (MCRD) San Diego, California

Very early on the morning of 9 September 1965, I said goodbye to my parents. I told them I would write and send them my address as soon as I could. Don Caouette's brother Phil drove the three of us to the Los Angeles Induction Center and we traveled to San Diego on a Greyhound bus.

Marine Corps Recruit Depot, San Diego, California (MCRD)

We were told upon arrival to stand at attention out front of the bus station and someone would pick us up. Lots of draftees heading to the Army yelled at us, "What are you all doing over there standing at attention?" – but they didn't know we had joined the Marines. What eventually drove up in front of us not only shocked us, but seemed to shock everyone at the bus station. It was called a Cattle Car, and it was just a big trailer with wooden bench seats to haul people around. I remember the ride being very uncomfortable. An older Marine got out of the truck and walked over to us. Nobody was talking as he took our orders and told us to walk over and get into the trailer. Once we were inside, he said, "Do not smoke and do not talk."

We traveled around in that Cattle Car to the airport, the train station, and then back to the bus station again. In each place we picked up teenagers who had also enlisted as Marines, and who like us were waiting to enter boot camp at the San Diego Marine Corps Recruit Depot (MCRD). The Cattle Car was completely full by 5pm. One guy next to me asked how that Marine was ever going to know if we talked or smoked a cigarette. Another guy nearby said it was the rules. My new friend said, "Rules are made to be broken." So, we talked and smoked cigarettes.

Boot camp lasted for twelve weeks, and it was a long, hard, and rough time. There was a lot of "hands on" in boot camp in those days. Their

The "cattle car". (dustyfile.com)

Marine Corps' "hands" are "on" you, and they are not on you for healing. The Drill Instructors were there to turn teenagers into Marines. They preyed on 17 to 19-year-olds. When we arrived, I asked, "Where are all the adults?" The response was, "Shut up and get on those yellow footprints!"

Right: The interior of the cattle car that picked us up in front of the bus station. (dustyfile.com)

Below: The three of us – Larry, Brad and Don, with the three of the Drill Instructors: Sergeant Sloan, Sergeant Thompson, and Corporal Zavala.

The Marines wanted to turn us teenagers into killing machines. They wanted us firing those rifles when we met the enemy. Everything in boot camp was about killing. You do not just hurt somebody, you kill them. They write that on your heart and soul.

After getting paperwork completed, getting our haircuts, hitting the showers, being issued new uniforms, and making our beds, it was 0100 hours (which is 1:00 am for non-military people). We finally got to go to bed. We were woken up at 0500 hours by the shouts of instructors, and we all jumped up holding our bed sheets, one in each hand – over our heads. The Drill Instructors were looking for bedwetters. The Drill Instructors come in swinging, and they punched the biggest and tallest guys. I was glad I'm only 5ft 10in, because there were lots of bloody noses that morning.

We were ordered to quickly make our beds up and to get outside and count off. We all had a number written on our bare chests with a black marker. They wanted to make sure everyone was still here. There were eighty of us and I was number forty-six. We were just a number to those drill instructors. We started out doing pushups, sit-ups and other calisthenics, then we were put to work cleaning up the area the Marines call the "Platoon Street." The "street" was the area around the Quonset Huts we called sleeping quarters. Our Platoon had four Quonset huts with twenty Marines sleeping in each.

Now we were all very hungry. Most of us hadn't eaten since the previous morning. In the mess hall there was a big sign which read "**Take all you want but eat all you take**". I thought I would try the scrambled eggs, and I soon found that they had a lot of water in them. I put my tray forward and the server "slammed" down on my tray a load of eggs with his big metal spoon. He almost knocked the tray out of my hands. That was how they served us. He had a big smile on his face and seemed to enjoy the privilege. The servers didn't wear green utilities like us, they wore white shirts and trousers. I wasn't even sure the server was in the Marines.

There were fourteen recruits at the table, seated at attention, seven on each side on two hard wooden benches. We sat at attention at the old wooden table waiting for the Drill Instructor to give the order to eat. He suddenly bellowed "Eat that chow and eat it fast! Faster! FASTER!" When we were done, we were told to get up and take our tray and utensils and put them in in a stack to be collected and washed. Then we ran back outside and back into formation with the eighty other recruits that made up the training platoon.

The Quonset Huts that we slept in on Platoon Street in 1965. (Picture from my USMC boot camp yearbook 1965)

I was the last one still sitting at the table trying to choke down those terrible tasting eggs. From across the table Sergeant Sloan picked up a handful of them and shoved them into my mouth. I spit them back up and he grabbed another handful of them and shoved them back into my mouth.

I quickly thought, I better run out of here, because there are eighty recruits in the platoon and probably a thousand recruits that look just like me. I sincerely hoped the drill instructor would never find me. Luckily I was right. I bolted out the back door. There were hundreds of recruits standing in formations. I couldn't even find my own platoon. I hid behind a platoon of recruits and Sergeant Sloan came out holding that tray of mine looking for me. I saw him throw that tray on the ground and go back into the mess hall. I finally found my platoon and got into formation. I was safe.

Sergeant Thompson ran us out to the back of the base, where recruits were digging trenches about 18 inches wide, and 18 inches deep for as far as the eye could see. Another group of ten recruits were sifting the dirt with big screens. It was a hot, dusty day, and it was dirty, hard labor out in that sun. Sergeant Thompson then said, "This is Corrected Custody (CC). These recruits do not want to go along with our program. They will be here one week then they will be set back one week in their training."

I had to wonder what on earth had I gotten myself into. My friends Brad Begin and Don Caouette were in another Quonset hut because groupings were by alphabetical order. I had woken up to a nightmare of Drill Instructors beating recruits up, followed by a terrible breakfast, I had enraged a Senior Drill Instructor, we'd been threatened with hard labor to reward any screw ups, and had discovered that a recruit could be set back a week in their training at the instructor's pleasure. I had to wonder: what else could happen?

In basic training you could tell what week a recruit was in by his uniform. In the first week everyone wore yellow sweatshirts, with a combination lock attached and locked to our utility pants, and everyone was wearing tennis shoes. In the second week we were issued boots. After two weeks at the rifle range, you got to blouse your boots. This was achieved by a blousing band that went around the top of our boots and our pant legs were tucked underneath the band. In the last weeks of training and on mess duty you wore white utilities. After you graduated, you got to unbutton the top button of your utility shirt. We recruits had to endure.

After a few weeks had passed we learnt a few things about our Drill Instructors. Sergeant Sloan the Senior DI had joined the Marines when he was just 15 years old in 1950. He had served in the Korean war but hadn't gone to Vietnam yet. Sergeant Thompson had been a member of the All-Marine boxing team for two years. He hadn't yet served in Vietnam either. Corporal Zavala was the Junior DI. This was his first training platoon and

USMC boot camp, Platoon 179. I'm in the second row first on the right.

I was the first recruit in Platoon 179 to be issued a rifle. (Picture from my boot camp yearbook 1965)

he had just returned from Vietnam. These Drill Instructors were men, not teenagers.

Our platoon (Platoon 179) was in competition with three other platoons in our intake. We could win ribbons for our platoon's guidon. We ran

Platoon of Recruits on the Grinder practicing drill. The Grinder is a parade area that is paved with asphalt. (Picture from my boot camp yearbook 1965)

Bayonet training was always in the sand and it was always hot and dusty. (Picture from my boot camp yearbook 1965)

the obstacle courses, we drilled, we had to pass inspections, underwent hand-to-hand combat training, a bayonet course and pugil stick training, and finally we went to the rifle range. We knew that if we did well, the Drill Instructors could be rewarded too. We just stayed busy and ran everywhere.

After a couple of weeks, we were sent some recruits whose training had been set back for several reasons. Some were overweight recruits placed in the "fat man" platoon. Those recruits were just too heavy to complete the exercises that were required to pass at the end of each week. Some got hurt while in

Pugil Stick fighting was the closest thing to fighting the enemy with your rifle and bayonet. (Picture from my boot camp yearbook 1965)

One of the Obstacle Courses. (Picture from my boot camp yearbook 1965)

training, and some just did not want to obey the rules. A recruit could spend months in boot camp if he was set back.

Then we were sent to the rifle range for two weeks. It was a rifle and pistol range called Edson Range, part of Camp Pendleton where the 1st Marine Division was stationed. We were marshalled onto three Marine Corps buses. Somebody asked the driver if we could smoke. The driver replied "Sure, why not?" Everything was fine with the smoking until our bus passed the bus which the three Drill Instructors were riding on. They quickly announced that there would be two weeks of no smoking for the whole platoon. We arrived at a forming up point where several other

Marines from my intake marching to the Edson Range area. (Picture from my boot camp yearbook 1965)

platoons of recruits were unloading from the buses. We then walked seven miles in the deep sand along the coast. It was hard walking in the soft, deep sand with boots, rifles, and packs.

The barracks at Edson Range were unbelievably big, and they were also brand new. All eighty men of Platoon 179 slept on the same floor. The first week was just "snapping in." You pretend you have a loaded rifle and just practiced squeezing the trigger and shooting at a target. We did that over and over for hours each morning. I noticed several people falling asleep during this snapping in time. They also made us do a lot of running while we were at the rifle range. They also had a manure pit where we had to do push-ups and sit ups. It was nasty, and terrible smelling experience.

Shooting at Edson Range, firing at the 300-yard line. (Pictures from my boot camp yearbook 1965)

During our second week at the Edson Range, we started firing at targets from 100, 200, 300 and 500 yards away. We fired from the sitting, kneeling, standing and prone positions. Everyone was issued fifty rounds of ammunition. Each round fired was worth points, depending on where you hit the target. The bulls eye was worth five points. After a full morning of shooting, we usually headed down to the targets (which were called "the butts"). It was our turn to raise, lower, and mark the targets for the other platoon of recruits. All we could hear was the loud "SNAP" when the bullets hit the targets. It was like the sound of snapping your fingers.

I soon discovered that I was a fine shot. I scored 238 out of a possible 250 points in boot camp on pre-qualification day using the M-14 rifle. My Senior

A recruit marking a target in the Butts. (Picture from my boot camp yearbook 1965)

Drill Instructor Sergeant Sloan, whom we had not seen in two weeks at that point, told me to change some elevation on my rifle and I would break the range record. I made the change, but I dropped eighteen points to score 220 points, my final score. This was still an expert qualification, but the score was not as high as I could have fired.

In later years I thought about that marksmanship score. I truly believe that God was in control and that He did me right by making sure I didn't score any higher. It might have meant sniper school, a job I absolutely did not want. Snipers have a lonely job, and sniping involves too much waiting and lying motionless in the jungle or on an outpost.

We left Edson rifle range and headed back to MCRD, San Diego to finish our training and to become Marines. We eventually had our final physical fitness tests. This required carrying packs, helmets, and rifles while running the combat readiness course. One recruit who had been set back one week in his training from another Platoon had to run this course with us. He just had to jump over a 5ft-wide ditch that was about 4ft deep. We all watched and cheered for him as he ran and jumped over those 5ft. He went right into the ditch, but his head hit the other side. His helmet flew off and landed on the opposite side. All of us looked wide-eyed at the Drill Instructor. The

Private Larry Hilton USMC. MCRD, San Diego, California.

Above left: A smoking lamp that produces Soot to darken the front and rear sights on our rifle. It helped to eliminate the glare on the sights.

Above right: Private Dan Gibson getting his rear sights blackened. (Courtesy Dan Gibson)

Drill Instructor said he passed, because his head hit the other side. Several ran over and pulled the poor recruit out of the ditch and congratulated him.

Our training was cut short by two weeks. We got away without the usual week of mess duty or week of guard duty. They extended the training each day by a couple of hours, and we did some guard duty just to give us an idea of what it would be like.

Platoon 179 graduated on 7 November 1965 with four other platoons. There was a big celebration. Our family and friends came to see the graduation. My parents came and it was wonderful to see them. After a full day consisting of a graduation ceremony, lunch, and visiting, all of the families and friends left to head back to their homes. We packed up and got ready to leave MCRD. Sergeant Sloan gave me a small oil pot that produced soot to blacken our sights on the rifles. He said because I got a high score he wanted me to have this. I thanked him, but when he walked away I gave it away, because it was too messy with oil and soot to put in my sea-bag.

The Drill Instructors gathered everyone together and started handing out our MOSs. I was assigned the MOS 0811 Field Artillery Cannoneer. There were a hundred different Military Occupational Specialties in the Marines:

truck drivers, tank crewmen, aviation, radiomen, supply, machine gunners, cooks and so on. I was excited about getting artillery. I did not even know at that time that the Marines had artillery. I thought everyone was infantry.

I also thought we were going home on leave after boot camp, but instead we were sent to complete two weeks in the Infantry Training Regiment (ITR), which I was looking forward to. I had joined the Marines with anticipation of carrying a rifle. The next morning a few of us were waiting for the buses to take us to Camp Pendleton when we saw Sergeant Thompson walking toward us. I wondered what he wanted. He walked over to me and extended his hand, and said I did a good job in boot camp. I was shocked to see him and shook his hand.

I asked about what would be next for Sergeant Sloan and Corporal Zavala. Sergeant Thompson said they'd be picking up another Platoon and could not see us off to ITR. He said both he and Sergeant Sloan made staff sergeant (E-6) and Corporal Zavala made sergeant (E-5). He said ours was a very good platoon for them. Platoon 179 had won the competition at the rifle range, drill, bayonet course, and obstacle course.

My two friends Don and Brad (who the Marines were supposed have sent me through boot camp with in the "buddy system") were given very different MOS numbers from me. Brad was posted into a supply job for the Marine air wing, and Don was posted to the infantry. I do not know how the Corps placed people in these MOSs. Don, Brad and I talked briefly and then they got on a separate bus for Camp Pendleton. They were both sent to different Infantry Training Regiments than I was. I would not see Don again for two years, and Brad for even longer.

Chapter 4

Infantry Training Regiment

The Marine Base at Camp Pendleton covers an area of 200 square miles and has seventeen miles of oceanfront. I think there were 170 of us Marines that made up Infantry Training Regiment Company Q. All kinds of Marines with different MOSs were included in this training battalion. Without exception, we had all been sent to Camp Pendleton directly from boot camp. As soon as we arrived we were all issued with M1 Garand rifles. The M1 had been used in World War Two, in Korea and some Marine snipers also used them in the early years of the war in Vietnam. Our instructors were older marine corporals and sergeants who'd

Right and below: I'm in the front row, second Marine on the left. I'm standing by the Marine holding the flag.

served in the Korean war. None of them had been to Vietnam yet. They told us not to call them "Sir", but to just call them by their ranks. There was a closeness with these new instructors which we had never enjoyed with the Drill Instructors in boot camp. These Marines wanted us to ask them questions about the training we were about to given, and about weapons we would be trained on.

I asked why we were training with the M1 Garand rifle when we had only just finished training with the M14 in boot camp. I also knew we would only be issued the M14 in Vietnam, so I wondered what the point of the M1 Garand training was. The answer was simply that there were not enough M14 rifles to go around. The sergeant seemed surprised and asked why would anyone want the M14? I had developed quite an affection for the M14; it had a 20-round detachable magazine, it had a higher rate of fire and it even had a select fire switch which turned it into an automatic rifle. It was a weapon I already loved. After a class on the M1 Garand rifle, we hiked out several miles with helmets, packs, and M1 rifles to an open area where a truck arrived. The driver pushed off several large cases of .30 caliber M1 ammunition. Each of the cases held thousands

An 8-round en-bloc clip of 30-06 M1 ammunition. You loaded the clip by pushing it into the top of the rifle. Just watch out that you do NOT get your thumb caught in the chamber when loading. It hurts, and that is called an "M1 Thumb", or "Garand Thumb". Look on YouTube "How NOT to load an M1 Garand." When the last round had been fired, the empty clip was ejected from the rifle.

of rounds. The driver told us to shoot all of the ammunition and he would bring us back lunch.

We fired off those .30 caliber rounds for hours familiarizing ourselves with the M1 Garand. When we were done, we cleaned up the empty brass cartridges and had them ready for the truck driver to haul back to the main base. Then we ate lunch and hiked back to the barracks, where we cleaned our rifles, and then went on leave for the evening.

One of the hills at Camp Pendleton was semi-officially baptized "The Matterhorn," but in my time there the Marines had other, unmentionable names for it. We were in good physical condition already but we were made stronger by hiking over the steep hills at Camp Pendleton. We fired, disassembled, and reassembled all kinds of weapons. There were machine guns, flame throwers, rifles, and pistols. We even threw hand grenades. If it was a weapon that American troops carried on a battlefield, we fired it and cleaned it. It was all part of gaining experience and our training. I can especially recall how we spent countless hours training in the rain. "If it's not raining, it's not training," we often said.

After we finished two weeks of ITR training, I again began to think that we were going to have a chance to go home on leave. Unfortunately for me, I soon found out that I had two more weeks of training, and this time I was bound for the artillery school at Camp Pendleton. This was located on a different part of the large Camp Pendleton base complex that I was already training on.

The Matterhorn, Camp Pendleton, California.

Chapter 5

Artillery School

"FIRE MISSION!"
"Shell: HE"
"Fuse: PD"
"Powder: Full Charge"
"Defection: 535"
"Quadrant: 455"
"Stand by-"
"FIRE!"

When cannoneers heard "FIRE MISSION", we stopped whatever we were doing and ran to the howitzer we were assigned to. Marine infantry

M101A1 105mm howitzer.

in the field would call in supporting fire from Marine artillery. There were eight of us crewing the M101A1 105mm howitzer in Artillery School and we took turns being the Section Chief, the gunner, the loader, and setting up the ammunition. Repeatedly, the instructor yelled, "FIRE MISSION" and we ran through the exercise. We were soon firing the 105mm howitzers with live ammunition. We learned about using the sights and setting up the 105mm ammunition rounds from projectiles, fuses, and powder. I was made a Private First Class (E-2) when we finished that training.

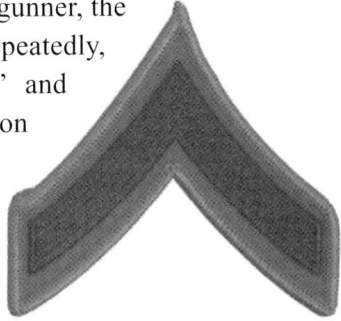

The single chevron worn by a USMC Private First Class (E-2).

A 105mm howitzer in the field.

Chapter 6

Camp Lejeune

As we finished artillery school, everyone was starting to wonder where their next duty station was going to be. I had joined the Marines to go to Vietnam, and WESTPAC (West Pacific) meant Vietnam. My orders had WESTPAC stamped on them, but this had been crossed out. The new orders read, "2nd Marine Division, Camp LeJeune, North Carolina". I went to a first sergeant and showed him my orders. He said, "You're going to the East Coast and on a Med Cruise." I was clueless as to what that meant, and just stared at him blankly. "You will love it," he said. It was the Mediterranean. I had never even heard of the Mediterranean Sea and I did not know where it was. He pointed and said, "See those two other Marines over there? They are going, too."

I walked over and met Tom Janeway but I cannot remember the other Marine's name. Tom said he had a car, a 1953 Cadillac. If the three of us drove together to North Carolina and split the cost, we could save money. That sounded good to me! First I was off for a three-week leave to my home in California and then I'd be headed back to North Carolina with the two Marines I had just met. And so home I went, and three weeks later I met the two Marines in Tom's Cadillac at the exact same spot where my Dad had handed me the keys to his 1950 Chevy two years earlier at the age of 16. Dad had said "Drive across the country, it's beautiful". I threw my sea-bag in the trunk and we started the journey across the country, and headed for North Carolina. It seemed the adventure of going to Vietnam and stopping communism would have to wait.

We planned to get on Interstate 10 in California, and then head east to Jacksonville, Florida, and then turn north to North Carolina. The drive was about 2,900 miles in total. We also planned to go down into Mexico twice on the way. Mexicali and Juarez were the two cities that we wanted to stop at, just to say we had been there. Those border towns can be dangerous, and we really did not have any business being down there. We made the trip very fast. I never had to drive so I slept a lot. I just looked out at the countryside as my two Marine friends drove.

When we got there, Camp LeJeune, North Carolina, turned out to be a beautiful place. It was January 1966 and it was cold at night, but the blue skies were filled with big white clouds. There were pine trees growing everywhere, and the camp's buildings were all red brick. It was like being in a different world compared to the West Coast. The Camp LeJeune mess hall had everything you could possibly want to eat. For breakfast there were omelets, French toast, pancakes, and all the white or chocolate milk you could drink. We were beginning to feel like Marines, not recruits. The United States Marine Corps kept a force of about a thousand Marines in the Mediterranean Sea area all year-round. That was just in case they were needed in that part of the world. Every Marine it seemed, wanted to go on a Mediterranean cruise – that is except for me. I had joined the Marines to go to Vietnam. I wanted to get over there and to serve with the first Marines that had landed there in March 1965.

I was by then a Private First Class (E-2) and I was put in charge of seven other Marine Privates (E-1) to paint the barracks and offices for the 2nd 155mm Gun Battery. The battery (and its six guns) was down south at Vieques, Puerto Rico, on a shooting exercise, and they were expected back soon. There were probably eighty Marines in the battery. I thought it would be an easy place to paint. My brothers and I had helped our Dad paint our bedrooms and other rooms in our house a few times, and it was a straightforward task.

We got down to painting. While everyone was rolling and using the paintbrushes, a Marine Captain came in, walked up to me and told me to, "stop using the rollers." I kind of laughed, and he was serious, getting in my face and bellowing "PFC, stop using those rollers! Just use the paint brushes." He then walked out. It did not make any sense to me. I found out later that we were working too quickly. I could have easily thought of better uses of our time, like some type of training on the artillery or going out to the rifle range to sight in our rifles.

There was an older man on the base, a civilian who was a painter. He told me that if I needed anything to let him know. I told him one of the

Marines had spilled a gallon of paint on one of the desks and that we also had a mess on some of the floors. "Don't worry," he said, "I'll clean that up." After we were finished and the painter cleaned up our messes, those barracks and offices looked brand new. I thanked the older man that did the hardest part of the project.

The 2nd 155mm Gun Battery arrived at the newly painted barracks and offices, and I remember getting a lot of compliments. We were assigned to M53 155mm Guns, Self-Propelled, and there was a battery of M55 8-inch howitzers nearby too. The two batteries were in a separate barracks. To an untrained eye the M53 Guns looked like tanks, but they could not fire on the move like a tank. It is better to think of them as cannons on tracked carriages.

A staff sergeant (E-6) led the morning formation. He had a mustache and said that anyone with a mustache and a lower rank, would need to go into the barracks and shave it off immediately. There was lots of cursing as several Marines had mustaches and headed for the barracks. The staff sergeant also asked if anyone wanted to get circumcised. I laughed. Circumcised? He said anyone who chose to get circumcised would get seven days of light duty. Being circumcised used to be required before a man could join the Marines during World War Two – and he had to pay for the procedure

An M-53 155mm Gun Self-Propelled. Its gun fired a 97-pound projectile.

An M-55 8-Inch howitzer Self-Propelled. Notice the shorter barrel. It fired a 200-pound round.

himself. Fourteen marines marched over to the Naval hospital to get circumcised, and their seven days of light duty. We cleaned and guarded the M53's 155mm gun, but I learned almost nothing useful about that 155mm gun in the two months that I was there. The Mediterranean Cruise was not going to happen until April 1966.

It was great driving across the country, and being at Camp LeJeune, and being on the east coast for the first time, but my heart was set on going to Vietnam. I thought I was wasting my time being ordered to paint the barracks with a brush, and cleaning and guarding that 155mm gun. On top of that, being around a staff sergeant who had made all those Marines shave off their mustaches bothered me. They had rights, but why fight it? You could get put on a lot of extra duty for fighting to keep a mustache. I was starting to see a side of the Marine Corps that I did not like.

In March 1966, I walked into the battery's office and volunteered for Vietnam. The battery's clerk, a corporal, said to me, "I can make that happen in about one hour." Just that fast and I was heading to an airport flying back to West Covina, California, with orders to WESTPAC Vietnam. It was the first time that I had ever flown on an airplane. Tom Janeway's 1953 Cadillac had broken down and he sold it, so he volunteered too. We flew back to California together.

Chapter 7

Jungle Training Camp Pendleton, California

I had surprised my parents, but not really. They knew I wanted to go to Vietnam, but it was still a surprise to see it all actually happening. After some leave, a hundred Marines started jungle training at Camp Pendleton. Back to climbing that Matterhorn hill and lots of sleeping outside. One hundred Marines, all with different types of MOSs and assembled from several different Marine Corps bases, trained together for two weeks. The Marines had a big problem at this particular time: they were shorthanded in Vietnam because of the demands of the war. The Marine Corps shortened the training in boot camp by another two weeks. It was only eight weeks long. They kept the two weeks at the rifle range. I am not sure where they cut the other two weeks, but they found a way.

At this point in time in the Marines, sergeants who had seen combat were quickly sent back for a second tour in Vietnam. Corporals and privates were not generally sent back for at least eighteen months. The Marines also offered thirty days of leave for anyone who extended their stay in Vietnam for six more months. Marines had to stay one month longer than Army troops in Vietnam. A tour of thirteen months was standard, and by then the draft had started, providing men to the Marine Corps for the first time ever. In the Marine Corps of the 1950s a regular overseas tour was eighteen months' duration. This was shortened to thirteen months in the late 1950s. The Marines kept the thirteen-month tour in place for Vietnam deployments right up until 1971 when the 1st and 3rd Marine Divisions had returned from Vietnam.

During our first day of Jungle training, a hundred Marines waited in formation for the captain to appear with our orders. He duly told us we'd all been put on mess duty for the next thirty days. Mess duty sounded a little more dignified than the Army slang for working in the mess halls, they called it "KP" for "Kitchen Police". I think there were about a dozen mess halls at Camp Pendleton. They sent eight to ten Marines to each mess hall. That was where I met a Marine from Kansas by the name of Monte English. He and I peeled potatoes each night for the next thirty days. The Marines ate potatoes with every single meal, sliced, diced, mashed or baked. Monte English was just 17 years old. He turned 18 while we were in Jungle training

Monte English.

and was qualified to go into a combat zone. He had never been outside the state of Kansas. I took him to the beach, Hollywood, and brought him home with me to meet my family and friends. We rode the train from Oceanside to Los Angeles several times.

When the real training started, it was pretty realistic. There was a replica Vietnamese village set up for training. It was as if we were actually in Vietnam. Some of the Marines in my group had already been to Vietnam and this was their second tour. The veterans all believed that realistic training was the best thing, and they even went so far as to have Marines dressed up like the Vietnamese people.

A three-day escape and evasion exercise was another type of training we participated in. We learned to survive off the land. We were taught how to kill and skin a rabbit and then eat it. The instructor gave us all kinds of pointers. He said the eyes were good to eat too, then proved it by cutting them out of the rabbit and eating them right there in front of us. I guessed at the time that if you were hungry enough, you'd eat anything.

We were divided up into groups of two and three Marines. Then each of us were given a small bag of rice, an apple and an orange for a couple of days. That was all. We had to start at point A and walk to point B, which was several miles away. Other Marines would be looking for us and if we got caught, we'd be put in a prison camp. You learned to go without food and water, and not to get captured while out in the field. We saw the Marines looking around for us, but we just laid low until it was safe for us to continue on. Tom, Monte and I never got caught, but several of the Marines from our training group did. It took us two full days of walking and hiding to get to point B. I thought "Vietnam, here we come".

Chapter 8

Going to Vietnam

On 15 June 1966 at 03:00 hours, we awoke to a trash can being thrown down the squad bay where one hundred Marines were sleeping – and by lots of yelling. We were ordered to empty our sea-bags, which we had just finished packing the night before. The officers were looking for weapons and they found a lot of them. Many of my fellow Marines felt they needed more weapons. The officers found swords, shotguns, pistols, and knives. One Marine even had a hatchet in his possession. All of those weapons were considered illegal to have in a war zone to kill the enemy. It never crossed my mind to bring anything like that. I liked the M-14 rifle and the M1911 .45 caliber pistol. After the weapons search, we repacked our sea-bags, and then it was time to eat. We were bussed over to El Toro Marine

Loma Ridge.

Air Force C-135.

Air Station just south of Camp Pendleton, where we would fly out on a commercial jet to Hawaii and refuel.

The military had started using commercial jets to fly troops around because one year earlier at 02:00 hours on 25 June 1965 a US Air Force C-135 Jet had crashed. The crew of twelve, seventy-two Marine passengers and a Navy corpsman, took off in the heavy fog from El Toro. They flew straight into the hills of Loma Ridge killing everyone on board. The Air Force officers flying the C-135 had not been told that as soon as you take off from El Toro, an immediate left turn was necessary to avoid crashing into the hills of Southern California. It was a tragic mistake.

We all got off the jet in Hawaii and walked across the tarmac to the main building. It was hot and humid and several veterans commented that the weather felt like Vietnam. It was nice and cool inside the airport. Refueling was fast, and we were soon back on the big jet. We flew to the Island of Guam and we refueled again. Guam was used as a B-52 bomber base during the Vietnam war. None of the passengers got off in Guam. There really was nowhere for a hundred Marines to go like there had been in Hawaii. The refueling was done by Air Force personnel and it was fast. After that we took off for Okinawa to store our winter uniforms. We each received a second sea-bag to take just one summer uniform with us to Vietnam. These were in case we had to fly home for an emergency, or go somewhere on Rest & Recreation (R&R). Our autumn and winter uniforms were stored in an underground bunker with big heavy steel doors. It was a strange sight to see all those sea-bags stacked inside that bunker, as they closed the big steel doors. It would be thirteen months before I saw that place again.

All we took with us to Vietnam were our utilities, boots, T-shirts, underwear and socks. A Marine really didn't need to take very much stuff. We would be issued rifles, weapons, packs, and load carrying equipment (or "782 gear" as the Marines called it) at our next duty station in Vietnam. We should have received jungle utilities and boots, but they did not have any. It would be months before I was issued the jungle utilities and boots. The utilities that we wore literally started ripping apart as we wore them. The underwear was worthless in the tropical weather. Most Marines just went without underwear. There was a big shortage of jungle utilities and boots for the Marines.

"Old Shaky" was an Air Force C-124 cargo plane which had been converted to a troop transport, and we were to fly in her from Okinawa to Vietnam. The lower deck had four rows of web seats, two rows facing each other packed in like sardines, holding eighty Marines. The top deck had seating for twenty officers and staff NCOs. There was a lot more leg

From left to right myself, Monte English, and Tom Janeway. In the background we can see "Old Shaky" – the US Air Force C-124 which flew us to Vietnam after several attempts – in the background.

room topside; rank definitely had its privileges. We really got to know Old Shaky…

On the first day we were packed inside Old Shaky on the tarmac, the doors were closed, and it was June in Okinawa. "Hot" did not adequately describe conditions inside Old Shaky; it was something else. Old Shaky's engines would not start. Some officer finally yelled, "Open the doors." So, they opened the big front doors, and we all drew a sigh of relief and headed back to the base. More liberty.

The next day we boarded Old Shaky again, and again its engines would not start. The heat and humidity inside the cabin was starting to get to everyone and they finally opened the doors to let us off. I chose that moment to have someone take a picture of Tom, Monty and myself. The same thing happened again the next day, but a private yelled: "Why don't you get that thing started before we get on it?" Lots of heads came together and we waited. Old Shaky just would not start. And so we were given one more evening of liberty. And the pattern was repeated yet again on the following day.

On the fifth day, as we approached the tarmac we could see Old Shaky had one engine fired up with its propeller turning. We boarded and the crew started the other three engines, and so we finally took off on our seven-hour flight to Vietnam. Three hours into the flight, the crew handed out shoeboxes to each of us. They were packed with food. It looked like something your mother would have packed when you were in grade school. The sandwiches were cut in half and wrapped in waxed paper, there was fresh fruit, gum, and even a slice of pie. I yelled out, "We should have joined the Air Force!"

After we had finished eating, the crew collected the empty boxes. Suddenly, Old Shaky started to really shake hard, and the engines were really revving up loudly. I looked at the Air Force crew chief and he pointed to the small window. The left inside engine was on fire. That was a real sight to see.

The Air Force crew chief told us take off our boots in case we went down in the South China Sea. He said if we did go down, we would have thirty minutes to get off the plane. He then shouted that we were turning around and heading back to Okinawa. The Marine next me yelled out, "More liberty!" My first thoughts were that maybe I would get another very nice Air Force box lunch to eat the next day. Thank the Lord, somehow Old Shaky made it back to Okinawa.

We had to get more money for more liberty. On the last day they just let us go to the enlisted men's club and drink for free. Only beer for enlisted men. A few days later, after Old Shaky had been fitted with a new engine and as we started to board, an officer told me to go topside. I do not know why he picked me, and once again, I was separated from my friends. I sat between a major and a captain, "older men" who were probably in their late twenties or early thirties. They looked old to my 19-year-old self. Everyone on the top deck was pulling out reading material. I fell into a deep sleep.

We did end up getting that nice, boxed lunch again! The major asked me if I wanted my potato chips and I said he could have them. He asked me what my MOS was. I told him artillery, and that I had just come from Camp Lejeune. He was also stationed there, and he had gone on the Mediterranean Cruise. I wish I had asked him more about his career in the Marines. I'm sure he had some interesting stories. Once we were over Vietnam the crew chief passed the word that we would be landing at Da Nang under enemy fire, which required a sudden drop to avoid being hit by the ground fire. I just thought it was all part of the adventure.

Chapter 9

Welcome to the NAM

As we climbed down from Old Shaky on the Da Nang runway, the dust, heat, humidity, and smell were just unbelievable. I remember immediately thinking to myself that thirteen months in a place like this was going to be a very difficult time. Anybody who has seen the Oliver Stone movie *Platoon* and its opening two-minute scene can imagine what happened next. I, along with the officers and staff NCOs on the upper deck got off first. As we were getting off Old Shaky, I could see the Air Force personnel were simultaneously refueling the aircraft, checking it over for bullet holes, and getting ready to take a plane load of Marines back to Okinawa. The returning Marines looked like they had just been picked from the field. They had just finished their thirteen-month long tour of duty. No body bags were at the airport and I later learned that remains were sent home at night in coffins from Da Nang and Saigon airports, where the two mortuaries were located. That changed however, and I would see body bags at the Phu Bai airport later in my tour.

When we arrived in Vietnam we all were wearing new, clean uniforms and freshly shined boots. That made for a stark contrast with the Marines who were preparing to fly back to Okinawa. These poor guys passing us looked bad. All were very thin, very dark from the hot sun, and they all seemed to have a dazed look upon their faces. I'll never forget the dazed look on those Marines. We came to know that look soon enough ourselves, and we called it "the thousand-yard stare".

Of course, some of the veterans yelled, "WELCOME TO THE NAM", and they climbed aboard Old Shaky for the flight to Okinawa, their first leg of the journey back home. Our thirteen months in Vietnam were just beginning. One thing I learned quickly is that you had to put thirteen months of time out of your mind and stay busy. I never kept a calendar marking off the days until I started my thirteenth month. Somebody then gave me a thirty-one-day calendar, and I used it.

I caught up with Tom Janeway and Monty English at the airport, and they gave me a good razzing for having flown sitting upstairs with the officers. We picked up our sea-bags and headed over to a building and got checked in and exchanged our US dollars. In return we were issued MPC (Military Payment Certificates) which was the money that we could use in Vietnam. Somebody had all our records. Usually, each Marine carried his own folder with documents and orders from one duty station to the next. We were told that we would be assigned to a unit the next day. We were then assigned a place to sleep, which was in an old canvas tent with canvas cots for beds. There were no blankets and no pillows, but it was better than sleeping on the ground. Also, there were some sandbagged fighting holes nearby to shelter in, just in case the base was mortared. We were in a war zone, and we would be issued weapons and 782 gear as soon as we were assigned to our units. We turned in for the night.

When I awoke the next morning, my upper lip was swollen and my left eye was completely swollen shut. Mosquitoes had gotten me while I slept. One of the sergeants warned me that mosquitoes in Vietnam were so big that "they could rape a turkey". He sent me off to sickbay to see a Navy corpsman. The first thing that the corpsman asked me was, "Did you sleep under a mosquito net?"

I explained that I had not even been offered a blanket, let alone a mosquito net. The corpsman told me I would be issued one when I was assigned to my next outfit. For now, there was not much he could do for me, other than provide me a bottle of bug repellent for future use. I then walked to the mess hall, hoping to catch up with Monte and Tom, but everyone had already been fed and now the mess hall was closed. The other new arrivals had already been assigned to work parties. There was much work to do around the Da Nang Air Base, and the staff NCOs did not let Marine privates sit around.

A sergeant soon saw me standing there alone, and he pointed at me and ordered me to go over to the general's tent. Lieutenant-General Lewis Walt was the Marine three-star general in commanding the Marines in I Corps. The sergeant said, "The general is away, so go inside and clean the place some. Dust off the desks and sweep the floor. Come back over here when

Lieutenant-General Lewis Walt (right), commander of the III Marine Amphibious Force in the Republic of Vietnam, welcomes the Commandant USMC, General Wallace M. Greene on a visit to the 3rd Marine Division's headquarters in January 1967. (USMC)

you are finished, because you will be getting your orders and will soon be heading to your new unit." I went into the tent and got to work. The general's tent was small, with no luxuries. The wooden floor was made from planks salvaged from ammo boxes. The tent was divided into two sections. The front part was like an office with a big table and several chairs, and the

Lieutenant-General Lewis Walt in company with US Army General William Westmoreland and other senior officers. Walt, a conscientious commander who was painfully aware of the risks of spreading the Marines thinly in I Corps. (USMC)

back part was the general's sleeping quarters. The bed was covered with a mosquito net. A large chalkboard separated the two rooms.

What was on the chalkboard was what caught my eye. General Walt had listed all the Marine casualties sustained up to that point in June 1966. I was just beside myself when I read how many Marines had been killed up to that date. Listed on the left side of the chalkboard were figures for all of the tanks, jeeps, trucks, artillery pieces, aircraft, and helicopters which the Marines had lost. Just about everything you can imagine was on that board that had been destroyed or killed by the enemy. I could see that the board had been erased and new numbers were updated daily. This was an eye opener for me. I couldn't help but think that we had lost a lot of men already, the number of killed in action being already over a thousand. That number has stuck in my mind all of these years later. I would go back to double-check that number many years later, and I found out that it was 1,260 Marines killed in action in Vietnam from March 1965 to June 1966. We lost over 14,000 Marines before we pulled out in 1971.

I went out front of the tent to smoke a cigarette, and eventually a big group formed. I walked over to the back of the marines standing outside another tent. My friends and several other Marines that I had been training with for the last six weeks were at the front. There was a wooden floor that extended out front of the tent and a marine captain walked out on the platform. I thought that several of us would be going to the same place.

The very first name he yelled was mine.

"PFC Hilton!"

The large group of Marines parted like the Red Sea in the movie *The Ten Commandments*. There I was standing in the back with a swollen lip, and partially swollen closed left eye.

I raised my hand and said, "Here Sir!"

"PFC Hilton, your orders say that you have been with the 2nd Marine Division in a 155mm Gun Battery?"

The captain had asked a question. I was thinking, *well yes, but for only six weeks … I do not know anything about the 155mm Gun. I was trained on the 105mm howitzer…*

"PFC Hilton, you're heading North to the Phu Bai airfield. There's a 155mm Gun Battery up there somewhere. They have taken casualties, and they need replacements. Here are your orders and folder. Take your sea-bag and head over to the airport and catch a flight up to Phu Bai. Somebody will be there to pick you up. Oh, by the way, do you see that second lieutenant over there? I want you to carry his footlocker and sea-bag and help him out. He's going to the same battery."

I felt sick. It was bad enough being in a war zone, 13,000 miles from home, but now I was being sent away from Tom and Monty, and all my new friends. I heard several guys say they felt sorry for me as I walked to the front and got my orders. I said goodbye to everyone and asked Tom and Monty to write to my parents so they could send my new address and we could hopefully stay in touch with one another. After that, I headed off to meet the second lieutenant.

Chapter 10

Meeting Second Lieutenant Upton

Second Lieutenant Herb Upton was standing by himself. He was a nice-looking guy, about 22 or 23 years old. He kind of looked like my older brother Ron. I introduced myself, but I did not salute (you do not salute officers in a war zone). Officers were allowed one sea-bag and one footlocker. I just could not imagine what a person needed with a footlocker in Vietnam. Along with my sea-bag, I picked up his footlocker and figured it must have been full of books, because it was heavy. He picked up his own sea-bag and his briefcase.

Phu Bai Airport in 1966. (Ralph Yarborough)

We headed over to the airport and got on a very small aircraft called a USAF Caribou, sitting in web seats. We entered this aircraft through a rear ramp. The Air Force Crew Chief folded up a few seats and placed the footlocker and our two sea-bags in the open space, securing them with some straps. We sat across from each other and were the only people onboard. As the crow flies it was only seventy miles from Da Nang to Phu Bai, and there was no Air Force lunch served on this flight. The Caribou headed onto the runway and climbed steeply away from Da Nang: it was a fast take off and a short flight north to the Phu Bai airport.

Second Lieutenant Upton and I got off the Caribou after we landed, and he went inside the airport to let them know that we had arrived. When he came back, I was sitting on a pallet of beer. It was made in South Korea. I believe the brand was "Crown". Marines were allowed two beers a day, if available. No hard liquor was allowed for lower ranking Marines. Most of the time in Vietnam the beer was hot. We really didn't talk much as we waited for someone to pick us up from the 155mm Gun Battery. Eventually an older Corporal (E-4) drove up to us in a jeep and introduced himself. He said the battery was about fifteen miles north. We piled into the jeep, and I sat in the back with the sea-bags and the footlocker. Second Lieutenant

Caribou aircraft. Roy Bell, my childhood friend, sent me this picture.

The Caribou was flown by US Army aviation companies when I arrived in Vietnam, but during 1967 operation of all fixed-wing aircraft were taken over by the USAF. Many Caribou pilots retrained as helicopter pilots. This US Army Caribou was photographed in Vietnam in 1964, during the so-called advisory period. (US Army)

Inside the Caribou. (Courtesy Colonel Patrick Hanavan, III USAF)

I took this picture from the window of the Caribou. It was hard to see out the small windows. But what I saw looked beautiful. YouTube has a video of a landing called Hue/Phu Bai Airport Landing-Pilot's view (1 May 1967)

Upton rode up front. Neither Second Lieutenant Upton nor I had a weapon, but the corporal had a .45 pistol, and his M-14 was in the back where I was. It was loaded with a 20-round magazine and with the safety on.

As we drove out the front gate of the Phu Bai Airport, we passed Marines with M-14 rifles and an M-60 machine gun at the guard post fortified with sandbags. They waved to us, and it was really beginning to hit me that I was in a war zone. We turned north onto route one, the only paved road in Vietnam. It paralleled some railroad tracks and I thought that it was strange they had trains in their country because I was expecting to see a jungle. The corporal talked as he drove us. He said he was the club manager. He ran all the errands and picked up the mail, laundry, and people coming and going. He also pointed out an orphanage on the roadside and said they did our laundry (and that it was cheap).

As we drove along I saw my first Vietnamese person, a young-looking guy, maybe a teenager or a little older. I waved and he gave me the finger in return. I was shocked and wondered if that meant the same in Vietnamese as it did in English…

I wondered to myself, do these people want us here? I didn't think he did.

The corporal said the 155mm Gun Battery and an 8-inch Howitzer Battery left the Marine base in Twentynine Palms, California, and loaded onto a ship in San Diego, California four months earlier in February 1966. They arrived in Da Nang by ship in March, after just thirty days at sea, and the sea passage had counted as part of their thirteen months in Vietnam. So, they would only really spend twelve months in Vietnam. Guys like me and Second Lieutenant Upton would have to spend the full thirteen months in country because we had flown over.

The corporal told us that the 3rd Division had a battery of six 155mm Guns Self-Propelled, and a battery of six 8-Inch Howitzers Self-Propelled under command. These were Fleet Marine Force (FMF) batteries equipped with specialized artillery weapons. Normally they were employed to increase the firepower of the 3rd Marine Division's attached artillery regiment (the 12th Marines). The 12th Marines were made up of four artillery battalions, and each of these supported a Marine Infantry Regiment. Someone in the high command had come up with the idea to join and mix the two FMF batteries and then divide them into three smaller batteries of four pieces to cover a wider area. There were two 155mm Guns and two 8-Inch howitzers were in each of the three understrength batteries. We needn't dwell on the understrength part, because more guns and more Marines were coming, as

155mm Gun Self Propelled in the background. 8-Inch Howitzer Self Propelled in the foreground. (Courtesy Ray Cochran taken at Phu Bai)

everyone was told. They sent one battery south to Chu Lai to support the 1st Marine Division, they left a battery at Da Nang to cover the port and its airbase, and they sent the third battery north to a place called Gia Le just four miles south of Hue City. Gia Le was where we were going. The two batteries trucks, jeeps, radiomen, mechanics, and Fire Direction Center (FDC) personnel from both batteries were then all divided up and assigned to one of the three batteries.

In June 1966 when I joined the battery in Gia Le, little did I know that we would not be made up to strength for six months. I'm sure the other two batteries had the same problems. I have also read since my days in Vietnam that other Marine artillery units were doing the same thing. We could not have known it then, but we were using the artillery to cover just about every Marine unit in I Corps. It started to make sense why I had experienced the start of that big push to train so many artillerymen a few months before when I was in Marine artillery school.

The corporal also told us the battery officers kept sending one 155mm Gun and one 8-inch howitzer and their crews on operations north, closer to the DMZ. These were for operations under operational control of the artillery battalions operating in support of the Marine infantry units in the north. Most of those units only had 105mm howitzers. Our 155mm Gun could fire a 100 pound round seventeen miles. The 8-inch howitzer could fire a 200 pound round up to ten miles. The 8-inch howitzer was extremely accurate, and its high explosive round was great for hitting Viet Cong bunkers.

When the two pieces moved north it cut the battery at Gia Le in half and this became a real problem, because there were not enough Marines left to properly guard the battery. The officers and staff NCOs started bringing in Marine infantry to help with the perimeter guard and to give us enough men to conduct patrols. Marines do not just sit around and wait for the enemy to come to them. Daily patrols were conducted, and each and every day they went into the villages around the battery.

We drove about fifteen miles and turned west onto a dirt road and crossed over a railway line. A Marine M48A3 tank was sitting across the tracks with the gun turret facing north. The corporal said we were just a few miles south of Hue City and only forty miles from the DMZ. The battery were firing in support of Marine Reconnaissance teams (RECON) who were not very far from us. They radioed in lots of targets for the gun and howitzer to fire on.

These targets were Viet Cong who had been observed moving in the open. The Marines had taken over operations in all of I Corps from the DMZ down to Chu Lai. It was a big area, and we had to make do with only two divisions. We drove between two villages. The corporal told us the battery was set up a few miles out on this dirt road. Gia Le was hot, humid, dusty, and dirty. It was an open area with rolling hills with clear observation for miles around. That was about the only good thing Gia Le had to offer.

Chapter 11

Home Sweet Home

We arrived at the battery, and several Marines came out to greet us, mostly for Second Lieutenant Upton. He got checked in first. After all he was an officer and he would be in the Fire Direction Center (FDC). I was just a Private First Class (E-2), and so the corporal said that I could possibly help him sometime with making his rounds. I thought that would be great and he showed me the club. He said they had the villagers come in to build it for us. They paid them for the building and we could use it for our allowed two beers a day, hot or cold. My impression thus far was that Vietnam was worse than a third world country. It was a very sad place, but I thought maybe we could make a huge difference being there.

It was still morning, but it was already scorching hot. A staff sergeant (E-6) checked me in. He was sweating so badly that he had to rest his arm on a towel as he was writing. Someone stopped and asked if "Kelly" was coming into the office since they had a new Marine for the guns. The staff sergeant answered with, "That's the plan." He needed help in that office, but office clerks were another MOS. I recalled that back in boot camp a drill instructor had asked the men in my platoon if any of us could type. I had told him that I could type thirty words a minute, which had not been enough to become a clerk.

The staff sergeant gave me the address for the battery and sent me over to the tent which house Gun No.3's crew. I looked closely at the address he'd written down. It said "Provisional Gun Battery". I didn't even know what a "provisional gun battery" meant…

The provisional battery's elements were spread out over several acres. The canvas tent where my gun crew lived was a long walk, and nobody was there when I arrived. I sat down and thought of my parents. I needed to write to them and let them know I had arrived. I was all alone now and would have to make new friends. Nobody likes being a newbie … and I knew nothing about a 155mm Gun.

Part of the gun crew came over and introduced themselves. I met Ken Marsh, Joe Leveber, Glenn Kelly, and a Marine who went by the name of Ski. All Polish or Russian guys that had names that ended in 'Ski' got called Ski in the Marines. They quickly pulled out their Purple Hearts to show me, medals for wounds in combat – something I knew I did not want.

These Marines had been sitting in a Deuce and a Half 2.5 ton truck as bodyguards for Captain Larimer – the battery commander – while he reconnoitered a new battery position. When their truck hit a landmine, all were blown out of the truck, and all were hurt badly (but not badly enough to be sent home). The exceptions were the truck driver, who never came back to the battery. Captain Larimer was horribly injured, had to have both

Gun 3's tent at Gia Le. Home sweet home.

L–R Ken, Flores, Joe, SKI, and Larry June 1966.

legs amputated and was sent home. The Marines eventually named the provisional battery after him. Glenn Kelly quickly asked me if I had ever heard his name mentioned while I was getting checked in. I told him that I had heard something about Kelly coming into the office. He was so happy when I said that, and he perked right up. He had asked to be reassigned and to get off the guns. He did not like being in an artillery unit.

Ski was just waiting for new orders. He had been in Vietnam for thirteen months with another outfit and he had extended his tour for six months on the condition that he could become a helicopter door gunner. One day later he would be denied that request, and he said he wanted to go home. "Smart man", I thought. Ken Marsh was learning how to be the gunner of the 155mm gun. Joe was the gun section's truck driver. Each gun had a truck and trailer to get ammunition and powder at an ammunition depot several miles away. I never saw Joe do anything but

Corporal Allan Lane Helicopter Mechanic/Crew Chief/ Door Gunner. (Picture provided by Corporal Allan Lane USMC)

carry ammunition and powder during fire missions. Also, when the gun and crew moved, everything would have to be packed up on the truck and trailer.

I asked these four men where our 155mm gun and the rest of the crew were at. The gun was only a hundred yards away, where Sergeant Likens – the Section Chief – Corporal Mullins and Corporal Flores slept. Sergeant Likens didn't want any privates sleeping with them. The two corporals wanted to be called corporals when we talked to them. "Come on, we have to fill some sandbags," Ken motioned to me. We were building a bunker to keep all the ammunition and powder in. We had a bulldozer that pushed up dirt around the gun to protect it from RPGs and mortar rounds. We also had a big pile of dirt to fill sandbags with.

The two corporals met me in due course, but neither man said anything. We all got to work filling sandbags and Kelly announced that he was going into the battery's office as a clerk, because "Hilton the newbie" had heard his name mentioned. Corporal Mullins didn't like that, and the two started arguing. I thought they were going to get into a fist fight. Finally, Corporal Flores said something, and they parted. It was degrading for a Marine Corporal to lose his temper. I was getting very hungry by then, having last eaten on Old Shaky.

The battery had a cook and hot food was provided sometimes, but not every day. Sometimes we all just ate sandwiches, but there was always hot coffee and plenty of Kool-Aid provided. The potable water came from wells and was kept in small tanks which we called "water buffalos". To render the water potable, it had so much chlorine added that you could hardly stand to drink it. Sometimes we just ate small boxes of C-Rations, which I always liked. After eating, the staff sergeant that checked me in came down to the tent to tell Kelly he was moving into the office as the battery's new clerk. I helped carry Kelly's stuff up to his new sleeping area. He was very happy to get out of that gun section. The Marine Corps actually changed his MOS, but he still had to go out on patrols and take his turn at guard duty from time to time.

At that time, we were being provided a steady stream of targets around Gia Le by the recon Marines. These stealthy scouts called in the location

Me after filling sandbags.

Above left: Corporal Mullins preparing to go on patrol. (Courtesy 1st 155mm Guns)

Above right: Second Lieutenant Herb Upton in the Fire Direction Control (FDC) Bunker. (Courtesy 1st 155mm Guns)

of enemy troops by radio back to the FDC with coordinates for the guns. The FDC Marines called the gun sections by a landline telephone and gave us the target information, including a description of what the targets were. Most targets consisted of groups of Viet Cong seen in the open. There were

Gun No.3 at Gia Le in June 1966.

lots of these targets, although I didn't know at the time that not all were Viet Cong. The farther north we went, the more likely it became that they were soldiers of the North Vietnamese Army (NVA) who had infiltrated southwards from the DMZ. It wasn't hard to find open areas because it looked like large areas of scrub and jungle had been cut down. We didn't know that the USAF had sprayed the whole area with defoliants like Agent Orange. The big self-propelled guns were parked in small gun pits inside the battery compound, wired all around to stop enemy from sneaking in among us.

I shot an 8mm movie at Gia Le, which can be viewed by searching for 'Gia Le 1966' on YouTube. The first thing you will see is me lifting a 97-pound artillery round over my head (below).

The first time that I met Sergeant Likens he and I were alone. His greeting to me was "Do you want to get out of here alive?"

I told him that I did. His response was, "Then do what I say, and do not volunteer for those patrols going into the villages."

The provisional battery had only been in its present location near Gia Le for a week, so the men were still building ammo bunkers, fighting positions, going on patrols, and putting out wire entanglements around the perimeter. It was a very big job building a defensive position, with plenty of labor involved. I learned how to build a good bunker and a lot about using and maintaining the 155mm gun. I think Sergeant Likens liked me because I showed interest in the gun, and I didn't complain about doing the hard

Me lifting a 97-pound 155mm round.

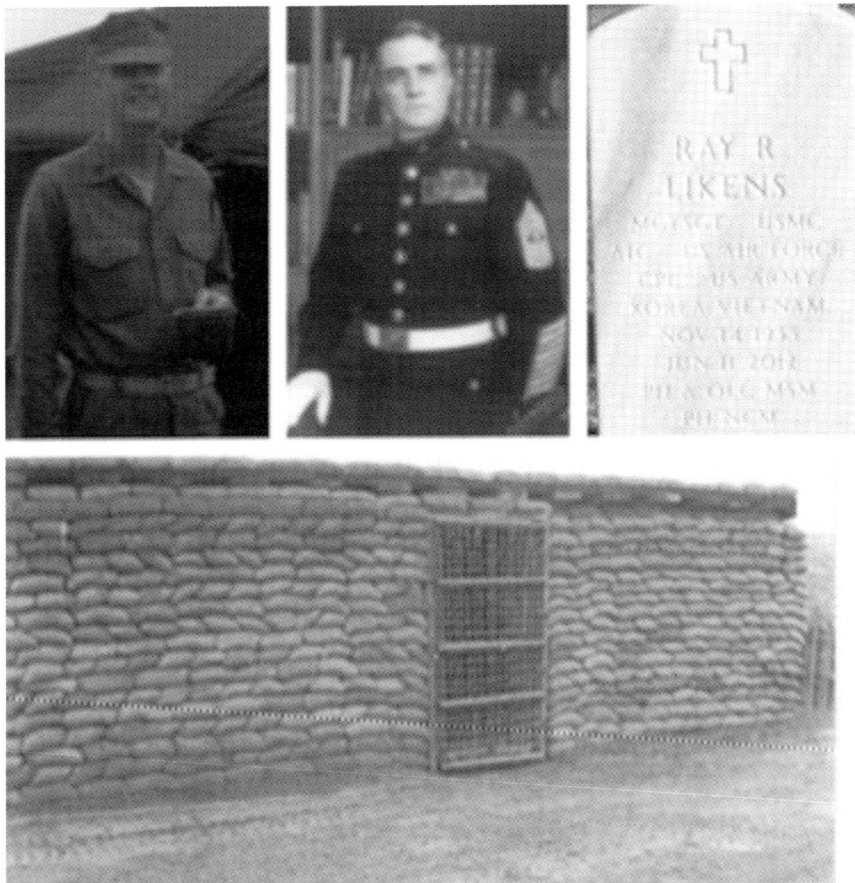

Sergeant Likens with his canteen cup of coffee. I have a photo of him in his dress blues and also his grave marker. The ammunition bunker seen here was the one I helped build when I arrived. Sergeant Likens taught us well.

work. There was plenty of stuff to do around those heavy artillery guns, and I just liked to stay busy (and learn whatever I could about that 155mm gun).

Sergeant Likens was in the US Army during the Korean War and had served in a 155mm Gun Battery. He had joined the Air Force for a few years after Korea, and then joined the Marines. He was already 30 years old when he went through boot camp at San Diego. He had seen a lot and we really laughed about some of his stories. He said those drill instructors were extra hard on him. Anybody who made a service transfer into the Marines had to go through Marine Corps boot camp. Ours was the only service that required it. The Marines do not care what rank you are or who you are. You are a private for twelve weeks in boot camp. If you graduate, the Marines will then give you your full rank. He was a sergeant (E-5) and he had all the dates and serial numbers tattooed on his arm from when he went into the services. He was a Marine's Marine, that was for sure.

Some called Sergeant Likens "Canteen Cup," although not to his face. This was because he constantly drank coffee, often in a canteen cup. He even ate the coffee grounds if they didn't have any coffee made. I don't think I've ever seen anybody else do that.

After I had completed my tour and had left the Marines, I tried to find Sergeant Likens several times over the next forty years, but to no avail. Then one day in 2012, I received an email from a friend with an obituary, and it was for Master Gunnery Sergeant Likens. He had retired in San Diego, California after thirty years of service in the Corps.

Chapter 12

First Fire Mission

"One round 100 in effect–
Shell HE–
Fuse PD–
Powder Full Charge–
Deflection 535–
Quadrant 459er"
"Stand by…"
"FIRE!"

The lanyard is pulled, and with a crashing BOOM…The big gun fires. The shock rocks the whole area, and you can hear it from miles away. I was

"FIRE MISSION!"

always excited when the landline telephone rang and they announced "GUN 3: FIRE MISSION!". (Picture courtesy 1st 155mm Guns)

When the Recon observers called in a target, they started out with a single round, and we then adjusted our coordinates accordingly. Then we would fire a second round and so forth until we were hitting the desired target. If they asked for a heavier volume of fire, we knew they had observed a larger enemy force. Sergeant Likens asked, "What's the target?", to which the FDC telephone operator replied, "A company of Viet Cong in the open." The FDC always informed us of the target description they had received in those days, but that ceased a few months later. It could have had something to do with security, but they never actually told us why.

By then Kelly had moved into the battery office, Ski (who had not gotten his request to become a chopper door gunner) had left. Ken was being taught how to be the assistant gunner, so he was up in the turret with the two corporals. One corporal was loading the round and powder and the was operating the breech. Our section chief Sergeant Likens was writing coordinates and taking information on the landline telephone from the tailgate of the 155mm gun. That left just Joe and me, and we spent our time running ammunition.

The 155mm projectiles weighed about 100 pounds each and it was up to us to get the fuses set up for each of the rounds, and then get the powder bags ready from their sealed metal canisters. The M53 155mm Gun Self-Propelled was supposed to be manned by a gun section of thirteen men – and we managed with about half that number at any given time. Sergeant Likens quickly asked for more people to come and help carry the ammunition. The one spare guy in the battery showed up from the communications team. Luckily for us it took about the gunners thirty seconds to load and fire that gun, so three of us could just about handle that rate of fire.

In the thirteen months that I was on those guns, not once did any staff NCOs or officers help us with the ammunition handling. Occasionally, any available Marines were ordered to go and help with the ammo when we had big fire missions. I'm not sure how many rounds we had fired when the gun started to really heat up, and that long 155mm tube was getting so hot that Sergeant Likens yelled for me to bring him a five-gallon water can. He had depressed the gun and then poured the water down the breech and into the barrel. It came out the muzzle in steam and hot water. I could see that the barrel was burnt badly. Those powder bags weighed about 20 pounds. That is a lot of fire and burning each time we fired. At night you could see the muzzle flashes from our battery for miles. We kept on firing, and by the time we counted sixty rounds, Sergeant Likens told the FDC officer that if we kept firing, the tube could explode. The FDC ordered us to keep firing. Sergeant Likens told me to bring another five gallons of water and I ran off to get it. We just kept firing round after round.

Sergeant Likens roared at the FDC over the phone that he'd seen 155mm guns just like this one explode from overheating when he was fighting in Korea. He was told to keep firing all the same, and then finally the order came to cease fire. I walked around the M53 to the front of the gun and saw that what looked like the rifling was sticking out the front of the tube. The muzzle was burnt badly. I called Sergeant Likens over to take a look, and he was angry that the FDC had kept issuing fire orders despite the danger to the crew.

The real problem was that we didn't have a full battery of 155mm guns and we were spread too thinly. We had only two guns, and the second M53 had been sent on an operation with an M55. So, all the firepower on that fire mission had to come from our No.3 gun. We were playing with fire continuing with a badly burnt barrel. A while after I left the battery on 13 March 1968,

Above left and above right: Here's the breach where we poured ten gallons of water to cool down the barrel.

an M53's 155mm gun did blow up, and this accident killed the whole crew of seven marines. It was a very sad day for 1st 155mm Gun Battery, but it goes to show what could happen if you didn't respect the limitations of the guns.

The 155mm gun was a specialized artillery piece, much longer than (and completely unrelated to) the 155mm howitzer. The 155mm gun could fire four different kinds of projectile. The most common was the high explosive (HE) round. The second was the white phosphorous (which we called the WP or "Willie Pete") smoke projectile, and the third was as an illumination round which sent out a flare at a given altitude which then stayed aloft on a parachute burning brightly. It lit up the surrounding area and it was intended to be used to light up the battlefield if we got attacked at night. There was also a fourth type of projectile which I never saw in Vietnam, a nuclear round. There was a special school and training program for that round, and nobody had the training in our unit. I understand the 8-inch howitzer had a nuclear round too.

I'm holding the powder and High Explosive (HE) round. Jerry Hunt in the background. A new Section Chief, but he didn't stay in the battery very long. The turret is painted white inside so we could see better at night when we fired the gun. It has red lights that come on at night. Still hard to see, but they tell us in training the enemy cannot see you. I always thought that if the enemy could see the gun firing, they could definitely see us.

Right and below: You can see the fuses in the top of the rounds. The fuses on the rounds are automatically armed when they are fired, making a 2½ turn twist as they go out of the barrel. That arms the fuse. It will explode on impact. We also had "timed" fuses that were set also when fired and exploded in the air before hitting the target. 100 yard killing area.

Chapter 13

Guarding the Perimeter

It was about this time that I met John Brophy, a new arrival like me. He was stationed on the M55 8-inch howitzer, and we became good friends. We were assigned guard duty together quite regularly manning an outpost with our M14 rifles and an M60 machinegun. The routine for guard duty was two hours awake on guard, two hours sleeping, so that all night long you traded off sleeping and being awake for the twelve hours from 1800 hours until 0600 hours. The battery was set up in a circle. The bunkers or fighting holes were about 100 yards apart on each side of our position. It was like

Outpost at Gia Le June 1966. Notice the open area, no jungle and rolling hills. (L–R) PFC Don Donche, Cpl Counts, PFC John Brophy, and PFC Ken Marsh. I was on that outer perimeter a lot in the first three months that we were there. Two Marines with M-14 rifles and an M-60 machine gun were posted. (Larry Hilton's photo)

that all the way around the battery. We had a wide field of fire for that M-60 machine gun. We could see for more than 500 yards.

One night, John Brophy and I were on guard duty in that outpost leaning against the front of the sandbags, smoking cigarettes and enjoying the evening. Out of nowhere a Viet Cong bullet hit right between us along the top of the sandbags. It sounded like being in the butts pulling the targets up and down at the rifle range. All we had heard was a very loud snap – we had not even heard the sniper's rifle go off. We ran around to the back of the bunker, got inside, and put our helmets on. I was beginning to take this war a little more seriously. It was noted in the battery's logs that, before I had arrived, a sniper had fired at the Marines and every Marine in the battery started firing back, out into the open area. Later, a patrol went out and found one dead Viet Cong sniper. Most of the time when I was on guard duty, I just sat beside that bunker with my legs crossed holding my rifle. If it rained, I put a poncho on. I also slept outside the bunker, just lying on the ground. When you're tired, you can sleep anywhere.

PFC Hilton

Above: PFC Hilton 19 years old. Tattoo USCM. (Larry Hilton's photo)

Right: My living area. We finally put in a wooden floor made from ammunition boxes, because the water when it rained almost flooded us out.

Above left: Joe Lefebvre, a Marine engineer (no name), Ken Marsh, and me. We are headed for the shower. Our shower was a big tank of water that had to be filled often, but when it rained, we just showered outside by standing naked in the rain.

Above right: Here I am in the enlisted men's club getting my two warm beers. Cold beers if the corporal could find ice. Most of the time I gave my beers away. I never drank very much. Across from me is Joe Lefebvre. He was in my gun section, and nobody seemed to be able to pronounce his last name. Next to me was a marine sniper who stayed with us for a couple of weeks, then moved on to another assignment.

Because only three of us lived in our tent, we had Marines coming and going, bunking down in the available space. We had a lot of room in that tent. One day, a Marine came to our tent wearing a .45-caliber pistol and carrying what looked like a suitcase and asked, "Is this Gun 3?" He said he was an engineer, so I asked him what he was building. He said, "I do not build things, but I do blow things up." He then opened the suitcase and pulled out a metal detector. He said, "I'm here to start sweeping the road from this location out to Route 1 in the mornings."

The Marine engineer let me play around with the metal detector. He also gave me some C-4 explosives. C-4 comes in the form of a two-pound block and looks like clay. He took the plastic off it, pulled off a chunk of C-4 and rolled it into a small ball. Pinched it and lit it on fire. He said we could cook and heat with it. It would not explode unless you put a blasting cap

Above and below: Our road going into the Village at Gia Le, where we spent time guarding the engineers. (Courtesy Glenn Davis)

in it. I never thought I would heat anything in Vietnam, but if you got wet enough and the temperature dropped, you could use the C-4 to heat up the tent to dry clothes. My mother sent me a camouflage rain jacket as the rainy season started. She wrote, "Son, it's going to start raining over there and you will need this rain jacket." I never wore the jacket outside the battery, but she was right about rain.

An interesting thing about Gia Le was that it was about four miles southwest of Hue City. It became one of the escape routes for the NVA soldiers when the TET was over in March 1968. They retreated from Hue City and passed through this area to the mountains inland. The Marines pounded them with artillery all the way while they carried their wounded, as noted in *HUE 1968* by Mark Bowden. It is a book worth reading if you want to know about that Tet Offensive battle.

Sergeant Likens had told me not to volunteer for anything, but all of us took our turn going on patrol into the village of Gia Le. On one such venture I noticed some US Army soldiers walking through the village. One was Steve Hayward, who had also attended Covina High School – he was in the class of 1964. What a surprise to see him in the middle of this village in Vietnam. We talked for a short time. He said their truck had broken down and they were walking south to Phu Bai. They were hoping to try and catch a ride en route one. I caught up with Steve years later and he told me he wasn't in the Army, but was in the Seabees (the naval construction brigades tasked with building just about anything). I also found out that our battery even had Seabees building bunkers, but I never saw him in our battery. Vietnam was an experience full of unexpected and random events like that.

A whole bunch of things were going on in Gia Le during my first three months in Vietnam, and I remember them as snapshots in time. In the course of my duties in my early days with the 1st Guns I went over to see the Marines from the battery communication section from time to time. One of the communication guys pulled out an old Colt Peacemaker .45 revolver – something out of the Wild

Steve Hayward.

West. We all marveled at that pistol, and everyone was excited to see it. We all asked the owner how he could have possibly got that into Vietnam. "It wasn't easy", the man said without elaborating, but he generously passed the treasured Colt around, and we all got to hold it.

Then we got an actual demonstration of that old gun's firepower. The owner cocked back the hammer and pointed the revolver at a helmet laying on the ground at the other end of the tent and fired one round. With a mighty "BANG" he hit the helmet and it went flying. Well, that demonstration was ill-timed because it made so much noise, that everyone came running (officers included). They took that Colt .45 revolver away and for the next two weeks that Marine had to fill sandbags and build a 3ft high by 50ft-long wall.

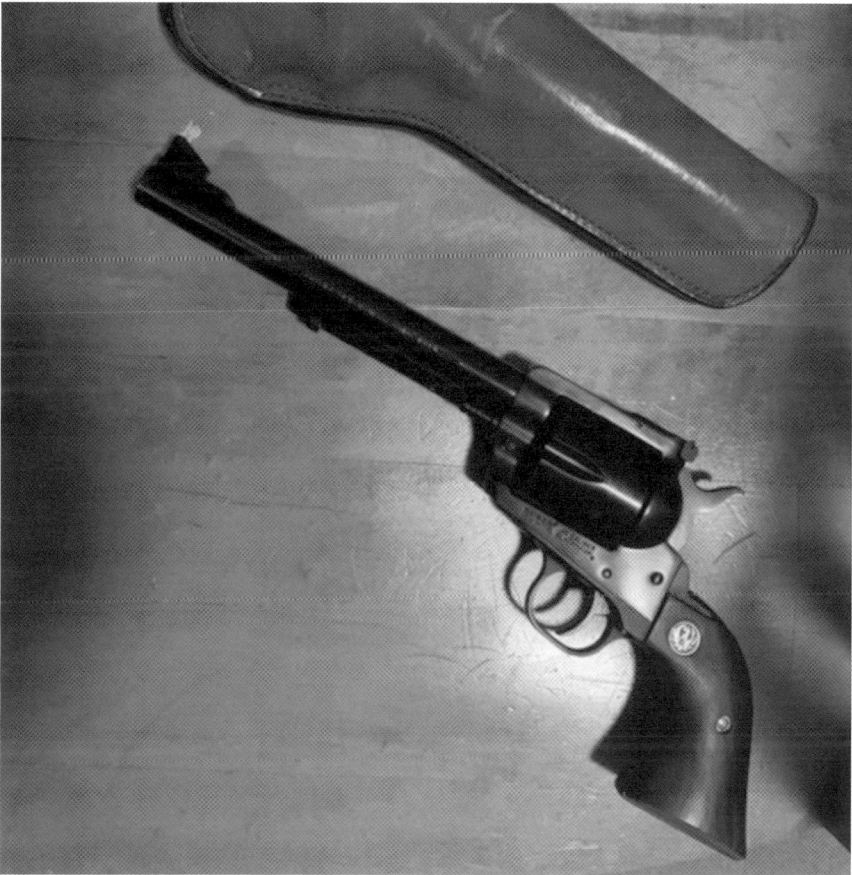

Colt .45 Peacemaker. (Courtesy Jesse Ray Baldwin)

After the morning roll call and formation, the name of a particular Marine was called out (sadly, I don't recall his name now) and he was ordered to burn the outhouse. We had a regular outhouse like on a farm, very small with two holes side by side. Later on we were provided with a much superior setup with two barrels half full of diesel fuel – made for us by the Seabees.

Burning the outhouse was one of the tasks assigned to someone different each day. The rest of the battery's Marines were kept constantly busy with security patrols, work parties, ammunition convoys and all manner of other tasks. Me and the guys from my gun were ordered to fill sandbags, and we got on with that when we saw some smoke over the outhouse – lots of smoke. The Marine should have pulled the outhouse off the latrine pit, poured gasoline into the pit and then burned the waste up. What he had managed instead was to pour a gallon of gas down the latrine and set it alight with the wooden outhouse still in place on top. Naturally, the outhouse went up in flames. To add to his woes, our Marine had used the outhouse just before burning it and had left his M14 rifle inside, and it burnt up. This man would also be filling sandbags along with the Colt .45 guy.

Not everyone had the moral fiber to endure the day-to-day anxiety of service in Vietnam. Another guy really wasn't doing very well in Vietnam, and

The outhouse we had before it was burned down. (mytrngdept.com)

something was really bothering him. He seemed to have mental health issues of some kind. Once our superiors realized that they had a possible psychiatric case on their hands, they sent him south to the Phu Bai "A" Medical Hospital seventeen miles away to be observed. We thought we wouldn't see him again but one evening, at 1900hrs, the sergeant of the guard came out to the outpost I was assigned to. He advised us that the man had escaped from the Phu Bai hospital and might be making his way back to the battery.

I thought to myself that he would have a terrible time trying to get back into the outpost, past all that wire in the dark. Unbelievably, that was exactly what transpired. The crazed Marine somehow got past the pickets and back into the outpost. He then grabbed an M14 and charged into a tent packed with Marines playing a card game. He yelled "I am going to kill all of you!", then cocked the rifle. Luckily the magazine wasn't seated correctly, and it fell out onto the floor. Before anyone could even blink the guy was mobbed by angry Marines, who beat him half to death. They tied him up and he was driven back to Phu Bai in the morning, never to be seen at the battery again.

Shortly after that incident, with everyone still on edge and nervous, wondering just what was going to happen next – another incident occurred. This time, some guys were playing cards again, and a Marine stomped into the tent holding a hand grenade with the pin pulled. He threw it in the middle of the card-playing Marines! They all tried to get up and run for cover, but many were knocked down in the scramble. The grenade was a dud and it didn't go off. It was planned as an elaborate joke, but nobody was laughing. A few of those Marines got hurt trying to get away. Not a funny story, but at least nobody got killed. That guy had to help the other two Marines build that sandbag wall for a long time.

Around about this time more Marine infantry battalions moved into the Gia Le area. Several more canvas tents were set up about 500 yards outside our battery perimeter. This helped us with effectively guarding the battery perimeter at night. We had these infantrymen visit our club several times. One of the "grunts", as we called them, went into the village at Gia Le about two miles down the road from our position – to have sex with a young woman. A Viet Cong threw a hand grenade into the hut where they were. The Marine and the girl were both killed. This was a big eye opener for us, because we were running patrols in and out of that village daily.

One rainy day not long afterwards two Marines were riding back from the village to Gia Le on a Mechanical Mule (which is a small, motorized vehicle the Marine infantry used to carry 106mm recoilless rifles). They saw what they thought was a fellow Marine walking in the rain and they pulled up to him to offer a lift. It was a Viet Cong dressed like a Marine – wearing one of our helmets, pants and boots, and a Marine poncho. The Viet Cong killed both Marines before they could even clue in that he was Vietnamese. That kind of incident probably happened all over Vietnam. The Viet Cong were evil. We also regularly had problems with the villagers at Gia Le. The only way to reach what passed for a highway (Highway 1) was by passing through the village. The villagers were putting coke cans on the road every night so that when the engineers came out in the morning to sweep the road, it made it harder to clear it. I heard my company commander tell the village chief, with an interpreter, that he will mortar the village if they continue to throw coke cans on the road. I was shocked to hear that from a Marine captain, but we didn't see any more coke cans on the road.

We started giving our garbage to the villagers. Each morning two villagers came to the entrance to our battery perimeter with a small, motorized vehicle. We had a full garbage can sitting out there for them. We had just put out the garbage and within a few minutes, two villagers had come out and were picking it up. Then we heard a bunch of rifle fire. We ran a patrol out past the perimeter immediately and found both villagers dead, murdered by Viet Cong.

One day a very young Vietnamese girl walked up to our outer perimeter and dug into the ground, planting something there. The sniper who was staying in our tent looked through his scope, but he could not see what she'd left. The Marine engineer and a few other Marines went out there. He disarmed a small landmine. It's likely that the Viet Cong made her do it. By this time, I had really started to hate the communists, and I had ceased to have any trust in those Vietnamese people. The lessons were learned, and the hard way for some. It's only by the Grace of God that any of us got through those thirteen months.

We didn't have time to hang around the Marine infantry very much. We saw them when they were on the perimeter guard next to us, or if they came into our club. We could see a lot of tents being set up and we wondered what they were for. One day in July I noticed a lot of Marine sea-bags, stacked up like cordwood with white Xs painted on the bottom panel. I asked one of the sergeants what the "X" meant. He said all those sea-bags belonged to 3rd Division Marines who had been recently killed. They had been deployed on Operation Hastings. The 1st 155mm Gun Battery (SP) had supported that operation throughout. Our battery received a Presidential Unit Citation for our part in that one. We supported so many operations, that we could never keep track of all of them by name.

We always sent one 155mm M53 Gun and one 8-inch howitzer M55 up north to Dong Ha to augment the M109s of the 4th Battalion,12th Marine Regiment (4/12th Marines – the 155mm General Support Artillery battalion for the 3rd Marine Division). John Brophy told me that once a very large force of Viet Cong attacked had their position trying to take out the artillery as priority targets. In that attack there were seventy-five confirmed Viet Cong killed. He said a bulldozer pushed out a deep hole the next day and that all the enemy dead were buried in it. There were no Marine casualties.

The Marine sniper and engineer who were living with our gun section in our tent were needed up north. The engineer gave me a camera before we parted ways. He said he didn't even know how to open it, and I soon found that I couldn't open it either. I took it over to the club later, knowing I was bound to find somebody that knew something about cameras. Sure enough, a Marine showed me how to open it and load it with 35mm film. He identified it as a "half frame camera"; meaning it could take twice as many pictures and slides too. If you bought a roll of film with thirty-six pictures, this camera could take seventy-two pictures. I still have this camera today.

We had fired our M53s 155mm gun so much that we needed a new barrel. The gun crew could only perform basic maintenance: change the oil, clean the barrel, put a track back on if a link broke (what a job that was) and generally keep it clean. We also had a section of maintenance Marines attached to us who could repair the hydraulic system that traversed the turret and elevated and depressed the barrel. To fix that M53 we would have to drive seventeen miles south to Phu Bai, where a new barrel would be fitted. Sergeant Likens was up on the 50-caliber machine gun, Corporal Mullins was the driver, and he yelled for me to straddle the tube close to the turret between him and Sergeant Likens. I was supposed to watch for any snipers, or Viet Cong with rocket propelled grenades (RPGs) and to keep the Vietnamese children from getting run over as we drove down Highway 1 to Phu Bai. The M53 weighed over fifty tons, but it could motor along on a road at a top speed of 35mph. Riding up on the gun was an adventure, but it was scary too. I was on the outside in the open air, and it was nice speeding down Highway 1 to Phu Bai. I had not been back to Phu Bai since I had landed there three months earlier.

Ken and Joe drove the ammo truck and trailer and followed us. When we got to the mechanical repair station in Phu Bai, they picked us up and we

My 35mm camera.

drove to the PX. It was a small place. Then we continued to the ammunition dump and loaded the truck and trailer up with 155mm ammunition and powder charges to replace what we had fired. We went back to Gia Lc and Ken, Joe, and I were put on patrols, work parties, and put to work helping the other 155mm Gun and 8-inch howitzer sections. They gave us all kinds of work, just about anything you can imagine – because we didn't have a gun to fire. Sergeant Likens and the two corporals just kicked back and waited for the club to open, hoping they had cold beer. If not, warm beer was ok with most of the Marines. It could be a few weeks before they replaced that new barrel.

Upon our return our new battery commander told me to go and spend some money in Gia Le village. We were trying to build relationships – in order to befriend the locals. I liked going on patrol, because at least we could get out and see the people, and more of the area which we were defending. I was always surprised to find how smart the Vietnamese were. Many spoke several languages: Vietnamese, French, English, and some Chinese. I started to look at the people in a different way. I never trusted any of them, but they were fun to be around sometimes.

My friend Jerry Hunt. This was how we moved an M53, with one of the crew riding on the base of the 155mm barrel. (Courtesy Jerry Hunt)

Our supply sergeant gave me boxes of M&M candy. There were ants in them and he was going to throw them away, so I took some boxes with me to the village orphanage. The children loved that chocolate, ants and all. I gave M&M candy away in the village every time that I went there. The villagers just seemed to be farmers like my grandparents in Arizona. These people were not that much different from country folk back home. I'm sure some were Viet Cong, but we all laughed and talked and learned from each other when we met. We hired one of them to be our barber. He did a great job cutting hair and it was cheap. He thought I looked like John F. Kennedy! I went into the village with a corporal many times to get laundry, get film developed, buy beer and even ice if they had it. He was the very same corporal who had picked me up at the Phu Bai airport back in June. We also picked up any newbies that had arrived at the airport. I asked if he could get this film developed. Sure, said the corporal. It was practically free of charge. No color, just black and white. In Vietnam we all had more money than we could spend.

Chapter 14

Moving South to Phu Bai

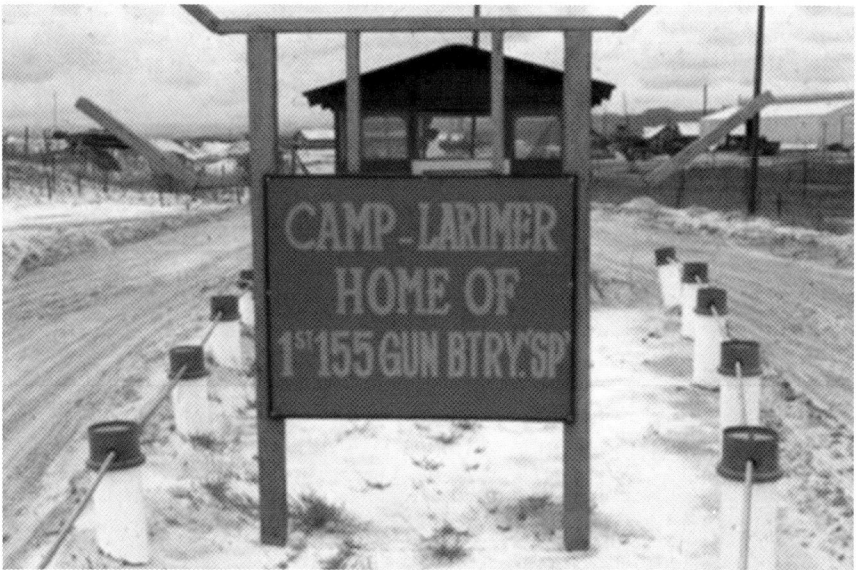

Moving South to Phu Bai September 1966. This is the sign for Camp Larrimer.

Later in September Sergeant Likens announced that we were moving to a new battery location just south of Phu Bai. I couldn't believe it, but my gun was still down at Phu Bai without a barrel available. We had been sending our M53s and M55s north to support the 3rd Division's operations ever since I had arrived. Sergeant Likens told me to grab my rifle and my 782 gear. He advised that the Gun Section would pack up the rest of my stuff and would join me in the new position in a few days. I was ordered to join up with one of the gun sections preparing to move south. I was also advised that upon arrival I had better get filling sandbags for a new bunker.

Above left: From my boot camp yearbook. A Marine's 782 gear and M14 rifle. The camouflage pattern on the helmet cover and poncho carried over from the type used in 1944–45.

Above right: Marine Flak Jacket in 1966. This thing weighed over five pounds.

All Marines carried their ammunition, water and other equipment with what we called "782 Gear" in Vietnam in 1966. The name "782" comes from the military form number DD-782. It included a web belt and suspenders, four ammunition pouches for M14 magazines and a pouch for a water bottle. The 782 gear was different from the M1956 webbing set that the Army guys wore for load carrying on the battlefield. We also wore a flak jacket in Vietnam, even though we had never seen anything like that in training. I was shocked to see the flak jackets when I arrived in June 1966. They were obviously too heavy and too hot for Vietnam, but we were ordered to wear them at all times outside the battery, and therefore we Marines wore them. Marines like to keep things simple.

I saw a 5-ton truck getting ready to head south from our Gia Le perimeter to the new battery location and asked if I could get a ride. I was told to jump aboard and so, I joined another gun section and helped them fill sandbags and stand guard.

The truck was heavily loaded with ammunition, powder charges, rolls of barbed wire, tents and the gun section's personal belongings. The whole battery moved out in column, some trucks even pulled two trailers.

This was a gun section moving on route one to the new battery location. There's a Gun up front, truck and trail with ammunition, power, wire, went and personal belongings following the gun. Some even pulled two trailers. (Courtesy 1st 155mm Guns web page)

We pulled off Highway 1 into the sandy area at the south end of Phu Bai. A bulldozer had arrived ahead of our battery and already had a gun pit pushed out for us. The section set the gun up immediately, and we started building the new Phu Bai base camp. We named the new base Camp Larimer after the first captain of the battery, who had been injured so badly that he had to have both legs amputated back in June.

The south of Phu Bai was on sandy soil but was also a graveyard for the nearby village. The Vietnamese cemetery was made up of many small graves. Because we'd chosen the area as a base, the villagers had to dig up the remains of their loved ones and transport them to another area. The local custom was to cremate the dead, so each grave contained ashes which were buried 3 to 4ft down in the ground – and they didn't use urns either. They dug down until they hit a layer of red clay under the sand, this served like a cap over the ashes which were buried in a grave underneath. They had to peel back the layer of clay, scoop out the ashes, and place them in a small box (which resembled a shoe box). The villagers would lay out a small cloth, and flip two coins as they were scooping out the ashes. It was surreal to watch them; the coins had to come up just right or

Above and below: Vietnamese grave diggers. (Courtesy 1st 155mm Guns web page)

they would continue scooping out ashes until those coins did fall in the right position. Then the grave diggers moved on to another grave.

We always sent a detail of three Marines to guard the grave diggers as they went about their work. Each morning we met them out by the perimeter entrance and we checked them over and looked at their ID cards. One was my father's age, born in 1918. Another gravedigger was in the habit of constantly looking around, which aroused our suspicions. We put him in a grave for the rest of the morning. Was he a Viet Cong? We couldn't know

Above left: Vietnamese Grave Digger at Phu Bai 1966.

Above right: Me, guarding the Grave Diggers. It was raining this morning when these pictures were taken.

for sure, but he kept looking at the M53 155mm Gun and around the area. We told one of our officers about the guy, but he said let him go. We never saw that Vietnamese man again.

Once the main part of the graveyard had been moved, the bulldozer set about its work, completely leveling the place. The camp was being set up so that the battery's 155mm Guns and 8-inch howitzers could move right into prepared positions as soon as they eventually arrived. Two of the 8-inch howitzers and sections had been assigned to support an operation up north, and our Gun 3 was still waiting for its new barrel, so that left just one M53 to support the Marine RECON teams here at Phu Bai. The battery Fire Direction Center (FDC) team was working out of a van filled with maps and radios so they could stay in touch with the RECON Marines.

We kept busy keeping the local kids away. The children from the closest village were walking around, and we tried to keep them away from our position. Finally, we started putting out barbed wire along the perimeter, and we told the kids to stay on the other side of that wire. One small boy walked over to the one-inch barbed wire and put a bare foot right on it, and just looked at us. His feet were like leather. It made me laugh. The perimeter was enlarged regularly. We started it in September 1966 and when I left Vietnam in July 1967 there were still Marines adding more rows of barbed wire to that perimeter. We needed to widen the Phu Bai perimeter to improve our security.

The village girls stopped by the perimeter often when we first arrived. With no wire to keep them out in the early days, Marines were meeting up with the girls and exchanging C-rations for sex. We were warned to stay away from the local women because of the risk of catching sexually transmitted diseases. We never let any Vietnamese girls inside the base camp for this reason. Many American units would pay a terrible price for letting the young girls and barbers into their base camps, because some of them were Viet Cong. To us the Vietnamese all looked alike. The farmers, women, young girls and boys all could be Viet Cong and nobody ever knew until it was too late. I never trusted any of these people.

Even though the Phu Bai graveyard had for the most part been moved at Camp Larimer, there were still plenty of big family graves left in areas

Two suspected Viet Cong captives at Dong Ha. (Picture courtesy Mike Wilson)

Three of the 155mm Guns firing. Notice how open the area was at Phu Bai in 1966. Also, the mountain range in the background. (Courtesy 1st 155mm Guns web page)

where there was no "military" reasons for moving them. This posed a real problem because we were under sniper fire very often. It's hard to spot a sniper in a graveyard full of headstones. I walked out among the graves by myself once with my M-14, and it felt very uncomfortable. I took pictures of the graves, and I was pretty far from the battery. I got a creepy feeling suddenly and it was just about to start raining, so I went back to the battery.

In the early days at Phu Bai we did not have an outhouse, so we dug holes away from the battery for use as latrines. I just happened to see some plywood laying around and one large piece had four holes in it. The five pieces of plywood was enough for four sides and a top with the four holes. I dug a big hole over 4ft down in the sand. An officer came over with a roll of toilet paper and said, "that's deep enough". He extended his hand and pulled me out. We quickly sat up the four sides that interlocked with each other around the hole. We then put the four-hole piece of plywood over the top of that. The officer quickly pulled down his pants and sat on one of the holes. As I turned to walk away, three more Marines came over and sat down on the remaining holes. Success!

We made urinals by punching holes in the bottom of metal powder canisters buried a couple of feet in the ground. We always knew when it

Right and below: Picture of Ray Cochran in Vietnam, and his famous latrine design

Ray Cochran in 2021, living in Florida.

was time to change a urinal canister when the smell was unbearable. The Seabees in the meantime were making a science out of building outhouses. They employed 55-gallon barrels carefully cut in half. The drums were then partly filled with diesel fuel. The battery eventually obtained one of these excellent latrines from them. The Seabee base was just a few hundred yards east of our battery position. I met Ray Cochran, one of the Seabees, online years ago. He said he invented the "crapper" we all used in Vietnam. He and I are still friends, and his story shared here has a certain pertinence to my own experiences as a latrine builder in September 1966. Ray drew up the plans for the "Phu Bai Outhouse" as a 20-year-old Seabee EA-3 in MCB-7. He still has the original blueprint.

> The MCB-7 commanding officer ordered me to talk with the battalion surgeon, who told me that any open latrine posed a serious health hazard. After that I designed an extremely simple building which resembled a run of the mill outhouse. The basic design was incrementally expandable from a two-seater to a eight-seater. My innovation was to place a third of a steel barrel under the "dump hole". Once "full" we could remove it; then stir it up thoroughly with diesel fuel, and finally burn it to a crisp. Needless to say, the stench of burning waste was horrible. Hopefully, the wind didn't shift when you were trying to eat upwind. Once MCB-7 had built the original to my design, the plans made their way up the chain of command. It was added into the Army Corps of Engineers' Standard Design Manual shortly afterward – and from there it went 'Nam wide.

All arms of the United States military used the Phu Bai Outhouse, it has been used in Bosnia, Iraq, Afghanistan and many other parts of the world where facilities are required without running water. A replica is even on display in the Seabee Museum in Port Hueneme, CA. Ray's lasting legacy to Uncle Sam was a stinkin' outhouse!

Chapter 15

I was promoted to Lance Corporal (E-3)

Latrine duty was the worst working detail to be on, but we all had to do it daily. I was promoted to lance corporal (which was the rank of E-3) in the next few days. I always thought my promotion was because I had dug that hole for the outhouse. I had only been in the Marines one year, but in those days, you could move up a rank very quickly in a war zone.

The rank of lance Corporal E-3.

Once the perimeter was set up we were ordered to get the M53s and M55s set up in their positions. The FDC bunker was being built by the Seabees. The gun sections built their own bunkers and fighting positions. Because the guns had to be protected, each gun pit had a sand berm pushed up around the position to make a gun pit. The surrounding area was strung with barbed wire around it for double protection. When the battery was being mortared, we could often expect a ground attack by the Viet Cong led by sappers. The artillery was the main target, and that FDC bunker was high on their list too. The FDC bunker was the heartbeat of the battery, with all the radio equipment, and all the officers and Staff NCOs inside.

Many people thought the North Vietnamese Army sappers who attacked us in company with the Viet Cong were some kind of suicide team. They called themselves sappers, but they were no more that the equivalent of what the American military called "combat engineers". The sappers were specialized teams of men who were trained to infiltrate into base camps. They would observe and position themselves around a base camp or an artillery battery, and when they figured we would least expect it, they attacked. The attacks always started off with a mortar barrage, followed by a full-blown sapper assault. The sappers were well-armed with AK-47 rifles, hand grenades, flamethrowers, pistols, and satchel charges loaded with explosives. They often wore a minimum of clothes (this helped prevent them getting caught in the barbed wire), just a loincloth. They tied their arms and legs with cloth strips in case they were wounded and could be more easily pulled out. Some even had a rope tied around them, so they could be easily dragged back to their field hospital.

Communication wire had to be run from the FDC to each of the guns, and to the observation post. The battery at Phu Bai was smaller than most and comprised about a five-acre perimeter. The Viet Cong and the North Vietnamese Army had every intention of finding a weak spot in that perimeter and getting inside to destroy our guns. We kept busy trying to keep the perimeter secure, but we had a pretty predictable routine. Each morning we stood to and did a roll call in formation at 0800hrs. After that the work parties started their daily assignments. There was fence detail, sandbags to fill, an armed patrol performed security duty every day, we had our trucks sent out on ammunition runs, we had trash pickup, we had latrine duty and "burning the crappers", etc. One M53 gun and one M55 8-inch howitzer were always seconded to augmenting fire operations. These excursions entailed about twenty-five of our Marines leaving the perimeter to crew the guns on those operations. The 1st Gun Battery was always under strength, but even if we'd had a full battery that would only have been about eighty Marines.

With so few of our own men available, we started paying the Vietnamese from the local village to fill sandbags. We had never done that before. They started in the morning outside the front gate, and we picked up the sandbags when they had a good size pile. We had them build the enlisted men's club too, and we were already paying one of them to cut our hair. We were very careful about which areas of the perimeter they were given access to. They were always restricted to the area outside by the front gate. They were never allowed anywhere near the guns or the gun pits. Our fence perimeter was carefully maintained daily. We put up a double row fence of barbed wire. We put hundreds of sharp metal rods into the ground as stakes to poke the unwary. We filled empty powder canisters full of napalm which could be command detonated with an electric charge in the wire, along with trip flares and claymore mines.

Carrying the serial USMC 213238. This was the M55 "Satan's Disciple", one of the 1st Gun's 8-inch howitzers at Phu Bai in late 1966 and early 1967. (Picture from the 1st 155mm web page)

Two Marines loading a 200-pound 8-inch High Explosive round. The Marine on the right lifting the bottom of the HE round was killed shortly after this picture was taken, during an attack on his position by Sappers and NVA infantry. (Courtesy 1st 155mm Guns)

We laid claymore mines, which had a thousand steel balls embedded in plastic explosive. Those could be detonated by a handheld device that had to be squeezed several times in rapid succession. Once a claymore detonated it sent the steel balls flying at the enemy, cutting him to pieces. We had guard duty on the perimeter all night just like at Gia Le. The watches were twelve hours, from 1800 hours to 0600 hours. We watched for two hours up – and then we slept for two hours, and it was exhausting. September and October 1966 just flew by.

More Marines were arriving, coming in one at a time. Several of the Marines that had been in the battery since February 1966, and they were starting to become eligible for rest and recuperation (R&R). An R&R trip meant traveling to another country for seven days of leave. This was well-deserved for those fortunate enough to be eligible, but it also left the battery shorthanded.

We had constructed a sandbagged bunker on top of an ammunition bunker. We had a good field of fire to protect the gun pit where we parked our M53. We were never alone in those positions. Rats had started to build homes in the sandbag bunkers, a problem shared by every base area in Vietnam. There were rats everywhere. Once I was eating some sardines on top of the bunker while on guard duty, and I set the can down. A very big rat picked up that can, and just took off with it. Another Marine guarding the place with me hit the rat with a pop-up flare and killed it. Snakes came and went too, as well as big centipedes that were eight to ten inches long. Those things were creepy.

Chapter 16

Weapons We Used

The Fire Direction Center bunker was the "heartbeat" of the battery. It was also one of the most stoutly built bunkers, with heavy timbers and lots of sandbags to withstand a mortar attack. We had a whole range of great weapons at our disposal in Vietnam. There was a sergeant in charge of the battery's armory, and he would let us sign out any weapon we wanted.

The wooden box in the gun pit is the ammunition box that I carried with me whenever I was on the outpost guard, or when I had to guard on the perimeter. I also used my M-14 to fire hand grenades when the machine guns were firing at mortar flashes. Some of the grenades are visible, standing up on the sandbags. You loaded a blank cartridge to fire the hand grenades.

Above: FDC crew after the FDC bunker was partly finished. Bob Simington is the sergeant in charge; he's the second from the left. (Courtesy Bob Simington.)

Left: A USMC battery commander from the 1st Marine Division uses a binocular periscope to observe artillery fire during Operation Desoto in 1967. This kind of equipment was used to correct fire by artillery observers. (USMC)

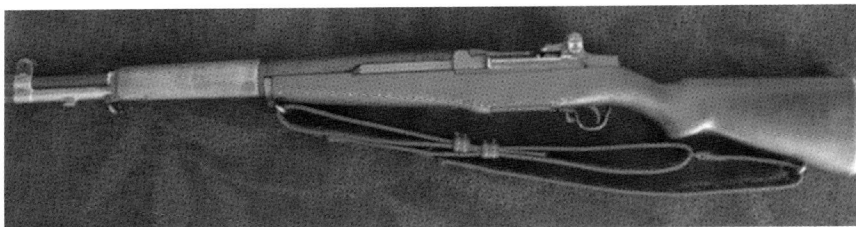

My M1 .30 Garand rifle. Fun to shoot but watch your "Thumb".

We used M18 Claymore Mines around the battery perimeter. They had 700 small steel balls inside embedded in a sheet of explosive, and when they went off, these flew out about fifty yards. An electric hand-held detonator was used to set the mine off.) (Courtesy Leon Powell A/3/187/101st 69-70)

Fence detail was an ongoing task, and our lives depended on it.

There was the good old M-1 Garand, which was an old gun but one we all knew how to use. As mentioned earlier, most of the Marines had carried the M1 in Marine infantry training after boot camp.

I often carried an M1911A1 .45-caliber pistol. It held seven rounds, with one more in the chamber to make eight. I thought it was heavy. One time in Vietnam a corporal told me he shot all seven rounds into the back of a

The M-14 had a twenty round magazine. It was a semi-automatic, full power rifle with a selector switch to make the rifle a fully automatic rifle. We also used the M26 hand grenade. I thought they were very dangerous. I never actually carried one while on patrol. In the picture above, I was getting ready to go on patrol and someone threw me this hand grenade. I caught it and threw it back, and said "no thank you".

M26 Fragmentation Grenade. (Courtesy Leon Powell, A/3/187/101st 69-70)

sapper as he was running away from him. He said the sapper never hit the ground. I told him he'd never hit the sapper. Somebody once told me that an M1911 was a great weapon to use in an elevator – at really close quarters.

When I received my driver's license from the Marine Corps in Vietnam, it permitted me to drive a jeep up to a 5-ton truck. They didn't have enough people in motor transportation, so they often made up the difference by stealing cannoneers from the gun sections. Several of us got qualified to drive. I was looking for something smaller to carry for self-protection when I was driving. I went over to the armory, and they issued me an M3A1 .45-caliber submachine gun. Everyone called the M3A1 the "grease gun". I only fired the M3A1 a few times, and that was just to make sure it was in working order. It was fully automatic, used a 30-round magazine – and it was fun to shoot.

We used the M60 machine gun frequently. We called it "the pig", because of its 23-pound weight. It fired a 7.62mm round just like the M14. It had a rate of fire of 650 rounds per minute. In April 1967, if you held a rank of corporal or above in the Marines, you would be issued an M16 rifle. They were new, and there were jamming problems with them. The issues were primarily problems with ejecting cartridges. I was issued one, but it kept jamming when I test fired it. I gave it to a private who was a newbie.

Here I am with my M3A1 "Grease gun" and .45-caliber M1911 pistol.

We had already heard bad things about the M16 from the Army. A story went around about a special rod being issued to ram out casings if they failed to eject. The rod was made up of three sections. The stupid thing was that they gave one section of the cleaning rod to each of three different Marines to carry. I couldn't believe it – how stupid? If the M16 jammed, and you needed to ram a jammed cartridge out, what happened if you only had one section? What if I couldn't find the other two Marines, with the other two sections? I guess I was skeptical, so I kept my M14.

You could also get issued with an M-1 Carbine. These were light and handy, and my friend John Brophy used one at PK-17. We had two M55

The M3A1 .45 submachinegun was used by vehicle crews, NCOs, artillery units and tankers in Vietnam. It was probably the cheapest firearm ever procured by the US government, with a unit cost of under $15 apiece. These Marines were photographed during a river crossing in March 1967 farther south in I Corps, somewhere inland from Da Nang. (USMC)

A couple of my old school buddies who ended up in the US Army in Vietnam. Roger Koler is holding the M60 Machine Gun and Brian Smith is holding the M16 Rifle. Brian Smith and I went to Covina High School. He was in the class of '64 and I was in the class of '65. Brian was a machine gunner, but he was made squad leader of an infantry machine gun section. (Courtesy of Brian Smith)

These Marine recruits are training with M16s in December 1967. Like any new weapon the M16 had its share of teething problems, and in its early days in Vietnam a lot of soldiers and Marines found it lacking in comparison to the M14. (USMC)

8-inch howitzers on PK-17, and this made it a very attractive target for the VC. When PK-17 came under attack John fired his M-1 Carbine so much that he ran out of ammunition. He started looking for an M14. John didn't use that M1 carbine again, he couldn't get enough magazines.

John also told me a story that we laugh about now, but nobody laughed about when it happened. John put on his cartridge belt loaded up with four magazine pouches filled with four magazines for his M1 .30 Carbine. There was a firefight and when the magazine in his M1 Carbine was empty, John removed the empty magazine. He reached for a second loaded magazine on his cartridge belt but he could not find it. He could not find his other three magazines either. It was dark and everyone was shooting at enemy sappers. Things were blowing up all over the basecamp and the sappers had overrun the position. John finally realized that he had put his cartridge belt on inside out and upside down. The magazines were upside down and against his body. He unsnapped one pouch and the magazine fell to the ground. It was so dark that he couldn't find the magazine. Finally, he found it, and he continued to fire at the enemy sappers, just as they ran right by him.

We had our own 81mm mortar at Phu Bai. When on patrol, if we saw footprints or baseplate impressions in the sand from a VC mortar, we radioed back to the observation tower in the battery perimeter, and they marked our position. If the Marines on perimeter guard saw flashes of mortar fire, they fired machine guns at the flashes. Along with the machine guns shooting, our 81mm mortar was also fired out into any likely area where the enemy could form up to help defend the battery. Each of the USMC field artillery battalions serving in Vietnam included a battery of mortars. (Courtesy Jim Kiser)

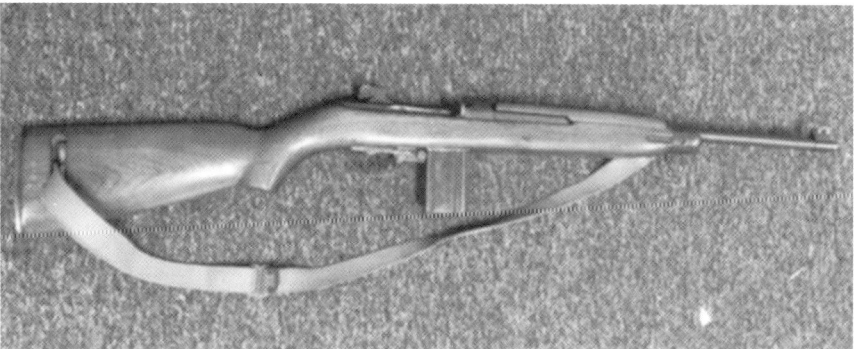

An M1 .30 Carbine, a lightweight semiautomatic carbine chambered in a special shortened .30 round. This weapon was developed during the Second World War and was still in widespread use in Vietnam. The M1 Carbine was largely replaced in the US Army and in the Marines by the M16, but the ARVN and Viet Cong used them right up until the end of the war. (Courtesy Jon Kennedy)

An Army M42A1 Duster at Phu Bai in June 1967. The M42 was sent to Vietnam to be used in a ground fire role, and we often had a couple of these attached to our battery. The US Army called these vehicles Dusters, and they eventually sent three artillery battalions to Vietnam armed with a mixture of M42A1s and M55 quad-fifties. We Marines called the M42A1s "tracks". The twin 40mm Bofors guns they mounted were the same "Pom Pom guns" that the US Navy had used during World War Two on its ships. The 40mm Bofors guns could fire 240 rounds per minute with both barrels. The US Army had developed a mounting for these on a tracked chassis to provide air defense for armored divisions. By the time of the Vietnam war they were still useful for shooting up ground targets. We watched them fire often. I went over to meet the soldiers who crewed this track. They showed me how it worked, but they seemed to be a little standoffish. They ate by themselves and they never went into our club anytime that I knew of.

Clip of the 40mm ammunition used by the M42A1.

One of the twin 40mm M42A1 Tracks from the Army's 1-44th Artillery at PK-17. The black soldier standing in the picture was reading the *Stars and Stripes* newspaper. He was later killed during an enemy attack on PK-17. (Courtesy 1st 155mm Guns Web page)

Every gun section had an M2 50-caliber machine gun. We put emplaced these on some of the outer perimeter bunkers at Phu Bai. It was quite a sight to see all the machine guns firing at enemy mortar flashes by night. The M2 was fun to shoot, and we Marines liked nothing better than to shoot machine guns. The rate of fire was 400–650 per minute.

Another contemporary photo of an M2 Browning machinegun, in this case mounted to the roof of the cab of an M76 Otter tracked supply vehicle. Photo was taken during Operation Onslow in January 1967. (USMC)

The M79 Grenade Launcher was a shoulder launched top break weapon which fired an assortment of 40mm rounds. We had two of these in the armory and someone always carried one on patrol. The second M79 went on operations with the guns when they were seconded to support other artillery units. (Courtesy Leon Powell A/3-187/101st 1969–70)

Chapter 17

The 3rd Marine Division Headquarters Moves to Phu Bai

One day in October 1966 after our 0800hrs morning formation, we heard a military band playing music in the distance. Somebody said that was the commanding general's band. The 3rd Marine Division Headquarters had moved north from Da Nang to Phu Bai. The band was made

Right: The Corporal E4 rank.

Below: Corporals Larry Hilton and John Brophy.

up of Marine infantry who protected the general. My first thoughts were of the blackboard in the general's tent that I had seen back in June when I arrived in Vietnam. I wondered what the number of Marines written on that blackboard looked like now. How many had been killed in action now?

We continued to send one M53 155mm Gun and one M55 8-inch howitzer on general support fire operations north close to the demilitarized zone (DMZ). At least twenty-five Marines had to go with those guns on their operations away from our battery. I was sure that we would be moving north soon, closer to the DMZ.

John Brophy and I were both promoted to corporal (E-4). We had only been in the Marines for fourteen months and were just 19 years old. This time a year earlier, I had been a Private (E-1) in Marine Corps boot camp. Now that I'd become a corporal, I got to sit in on the battery security briefings. An officer from division headquarters came over to our battery and gave us a briefing regarding what was happening in different parts of I Corps. I always thought the briefings were interesting, and I wanted to know more about where and when we would be moving. After the security officer gave his briefing, he asked if we had any questions. I asked how the US Army was doing in this war. The officer said he really didn't know, but that they were now up here in I Corps – and lots of them. I knew the Army was providing security for convoys going north and south on Highway 1. We had a post exchange (PX) at Phu Bai, and one day in October I saw several US Army personnel. Once while I was waiting in line at the PX, a US Army soldier walked up to me. I was surprised to see that he was a high school friend – Ted Busch from Covina High School. He told me his twelve-month tour was over in just twenty days, and that he was going home soon. I still had nine months to go on my tour.

Late one evening a 5-ton truck with thirteen new Marines came into the battery, all artillerymen, and all draftees. I was told to get them rifles, ammunition, 782 gear, and a place to sleep.

Ted Busch High School.

They seemed older, or perhaps more mature than your regular 18- and 19-year-old Marines fresh out of boot camp and infantry training. These men had been out of high school for a couple of years, not a couple of months like so many of us when we'd joined the Marines. They had worked full time jobs, some were married, and several had some college education. One man was married and was 28 years old. When these men were drafted, and went to the

Ted Busch in Vietnam in 1966.

induction center, they were put in a long line. The men were then told to count off, 1-2-1-2-1-2. All of the "1s" went into the Army, all the "2s" went into the Marine Corps. Boot camp for the Marines had already been cut back from twelve weeks to just eight.

We were all the while continuing to receive target information from Marine recon teams. A lot of the missions were for H&I (Harassment and Interdiction) fire. The recon teams would radio in the locations where they had observed Viet Cong activity, and called in one or two rounds on each request throughout the night. The firing carried on intermittently right into the early morning hours. A few of the M53 crewmen could fire the guns by themselves, but the M55's 8-inch howitzer fired rounds weighing 200-pounds. It took two men to lift those shells up onto the ramming tray. We must have kept half of the Phu Bai area up all night long when we were firing those guns. In fact, I have crossed paths with many soldiers and Marines who were stationed at Phu Bai in 1966–7. I have always asked them if our 155mm guns kept them from sleeping in those days. Everyone has remarked that we sure kept them awake. They all have a story about it and they all remember those guns.

Chapter 18

10 November 1966

On 10 November 1966, we celebrated the Marine Corps birthday. In Marine bases and camps around the world, there was always a big celebration every 10 November. The Marines have a cake-cutting ceremony and they find the oldest and youngest Marine at the celebration. The first piece of cake is cut

In 1966 our ceremony for the Corps' birthday was hot and humid, and even hotter inside the mess hall where we were waiting for the cake. You could see the frustration on the face of the officer on the far left, and the officer on the far right was wiping his neck. I was in the color guard, seen here on the far right holding my rifle. I was talking to Glen Kelly who was holding the Marine Corps flag. We were wondering where that cake was. It was hot and we wanted them to get this ceremony over with. (Courtesy Bob Simington)

and handed to the oldest Marine. He then gives it to the youngest Marine. It's a symbol of passing on the Marine tradition from one generation to the other. Every 10 November I'm on the lookout for a cake cutting ceremony. Once a Marine always a Marine!

The hot, humid weather was just a sign that the monsoon season was starting. The battery officers and Staff NCOs knew that three quarters of our battery was going home in about three months. They were soon completing their thirteen-month tour. There had been one month on the ship coming to Vietnam and twelve months in the country. The officers and NCOs wanted to know if anyone wanted to go home in time for Christmas. All we had to do was to extend our tour for six months, and we could go home for thirty days.

Only two Marines from the 1st Guns took the extension, and they were sent home on leave. One came back and wanted to go back home again immediately because of family problems. He was intent on getting his way! It was bad enough when we were being held down by Viet Cong snipers, but that a Marine would turn a .50-caliber machine gun on the battery and hold us down was unthinkable. But that is exactly what happened. This disgruntled Marine threatened to start shooting into the battery if he didn't get to go home immediately. We were pinned down for thirty minutes until a staff sergeant told him he could go home. We never saw him again or found out what happened to him.

The enemy developed some habits of his own in the last weeks of 1966. Every day, at around noon, a sniper would take some shots at our perimeter. The sniper must not have been well trained because he never actually hit anybody, but he pinned us down and we all took cover until he had finished shooting off several rounds. This sniper made his appearance again and again over several days. It was very hard to find a sniper from our perimeter because of the fact we had sited the camp in a graveyard and there were still plenty of big graves. The 1st Guns finally decided to deal with the VC sniper once and for all. We had two Marine snipers creep out into the network of graves at night. The next day our Viet Cong sniper started shooting right on time at noon. We took cover and waited – and after a time we finally heard one shot fired from the Marine snipers. That was now one dead Viet Cong sniper.

Chapter 19

The Monsoon Rains

The monsoon rains arrived shortly after, and I counted twenty-eight straight days without sunshine. It rained on and off until for the next few months until it let up again in March. We were constantly wet in that time and we got cold too. The temperature dropped from 100 degrees to 70 degrees and that really affected our day-to-day lives. After I arrived in Vietnam, I never thought we would need field jackets to stay warm, but we gladly wore them during the monsoon season. The rainfall brought flooding, and our base camp area was badly affected.

The enlisted men's club was flooded out during the monsoon – although this didn't stop anyone from going and getting his two daily beers. The effect of the flooding was pretty severe on lightly constructed huts and our club building finally collapsed. We eventually set it on fire once it had dried out. We paid the villagers to build us a new one in due course. I had my ways of dealing with living with the constant dampness. I had twelve pairs of socks. I cannot recall how I obtained so many pairs of them but I did, and I just kept changing socks. This was a wise idea, because wet feet meant problems. One day I went over by the medical area at Phu Bai airport and a whole company of Marine infantry were sitting barefoot on the tarmac. A Navy corpsman was dumping white powder on their feet. There was nothing worse for our troops than to have foot problems in the rainy season.

Being on the perimeter guard at night in the rainy season was worse than during the dry season, and it was generally a really scary experience. When it was pouring down rain, and it was so dark you could not see your own hand in front of your face, you certainly couldn't see an enemy creeping up. It affected my situational awareness. It was a strange feeling, because after a while in the blackness you began to lose your sense of up

Pictures of the battery and standing water during the monsoon. The water accumulated in huge puddles because the sand could only soak up so much of that water.

and down, or forward or backwards. In the two hours we'd be standing on guard our minds started playing tricks on us. We could never quite be sure if a Viet Cong was just feet away, or sneaking up behind, and the imagination would run wild.

The sights and sounds of the night would snap us back to reality. Suddenly the sound of a lighter was heard above the rainfall as someone lit a cigarette, or the distant report of a machine gun. We would see the red tracers. Maybe a trip flare in front of us was set off by a big rat or a rabbit (they were about the same size in Vietnam). There might be sudden brightness as someone shot up a parachute flare because they had heard something and needed to see what was out in front of them in the blackness. For a few moments our minds came back to normal. Those very dark rainy nights were the worst for guard duty.

I had to go on patrol on Christmas Eve and again on Christmas Day. The water was so high in the river by our camp that we had to put our rifles over our heads as we crossed. Leeches were everywhere in that river. They swam towards us and tried to latch on to us. When we got to the other side and climbed up the bank, we checked each other for leeches. A memorable Christmas for all who went on patrol in the rain and crossed that river.

Chapter 20

Becoming a Section Chief

Several Marines had been promoted at the beginning of the new year, but I noticed that I had not yet received any pay increase for becoming a corporal (E-4). There was never any kind of ceremony for my promotion, I was just handed the corporal chevrons to wear on my collar. I asked an officer about it. He counselled me not to worry and said "you'll get your pay, plus we're going to receive a new M53 155mm Gun and you will be the new section chief". I didn't start getting the pay for corporal (E-4) until 1 May 1967, so I was actually a lance corporal (E-3) doing a sergeant's (E-5) job for six months.

The officer ordered me to start building a bunker. I asked, "where's the gun crew for that new 155"? He said, "one Marine from each gun section will come over to join you." That was the same approach to manpower we had endured for as long as I had been in Vietnam. We were still short-handed for manpower in January 1967, but we were going to be a fully armed battery again at last. We would have three M53 155mm guns, and three M55 8-inch howitzers. It took the Marines ten months to properly man our battery. When the 1st 155mm Gun Battery landed in Da Nang in March 1966, its officers and men were told that more guns and marines were coming soon. "Soon" took a long time.

I was excited for my new gun and crew, and I went over to the new gun pit being pushed out by the bulldozer straight away. Now, I should point out that the "new" gun wasn't really new – it had probably been rebuilt several times. The M53 was a pretty old piece of equipment by the time I first received command of one. These guns had been designed for the US Army in 1952 and should have been used in Korea. They were based on the old M47 tank chassis and they used gasoline for fuel. The Army had replaced them with M109s (which were also in use with the 4/11th and 4/12th Marines at the time). The US Army always gave their hand-me-downs to the Marines, and that explained why we had the M53 and M55. The two self-propelled artillery pieces were pretty much identical except for the guns and mountings.

It was already raining and the Marines started showing up for my gun section. I told them we needed to put up a tent that I had received from supply. When we laid the tent out in the rain and started to raise it up, the ridge pole snapped in half. The old big canvas tent ripped in half and fell on all of us. I was the first one to get out from under it, and all I saw was lumps of five other Marines under that tent in the sand and rain. It was funny, and we all started laughing.

I had an ammo truck and told the section to climb in. I knew there was a Seabee compound very close by. We drove the truck over there, and an 18-year-old Seabee guard was at the open gate, standing in a small shelter to stay out of the rain. He just looked at us Marines and I nodded my head and drove past him and never said a word. I saw a brand new tent sitting on a pallet in the rain and told the gun section to dismount and throw the tent on the truck. We drove back out to the gun pit like we belonged there, and nobody ever asked us about the tent (but for the once).

After we got that tent set up and the gun section were sitting around drying off, a staff sergeant came over and asked, "Hilton, where did you get that new tent?" Before I could even answer he asked himself out loud "Do I really want to know?" I said "Probably not, Staff Sergeant." He just turned around and walked away.

Finding the tent had been what we'd nowadays call a good team building experience. Most of the new gun section did not know much about the M53 155mm gun. None of them had any training on one. They had been detailed on work parties, patrols, and perimeter guard since they arrived in the battery. I told them they would eventually have to go back onto work details, ammunition runs, and patrols, but for a short while we were to get ready for new M53. We needed to build an ammunition bunker. I told them that I wanted it to be big and tall so we could have a better field of fire. After it was built, we would put a smaller revetment on top and mount the .50 caliber machine gun in it.

There was lots of work ahead of us. To build a decent ammunition bunker, we needed more than a truck load of projectiles and powder. We had to dig

Ken Ed Joe Jerry Larry Bill

Above: The gun crew at Phu Bai. (Jerry Hunt)

Right: The bunker is high enough. Here I am at the top of the upper bunker. (Courtesy Ken Anderson)

out fighting positions in the sand that the bulldozer pushed up, and we had to string lots of wire around the gun pit perimeter to keep the Viet Cong from destroying the gun if our battery perimeter was ever breached. I told the section members that I could teach them about the gun itself and how to fire it by themselves during the Harassment and Interdiction (H&I) fire

The floor we built for the new ammunition bunker.

We had a lot of sandbags to fill to finish that bunker. In the foreground we can see the 155mm gun barrel on the M53 named "Bad News".

missions the RECON teams would ask us for. But first, we needed to work together to get a safe position ready.

I decided I would also sleep in the same tent as the rest of the new gun section. I felt that was very important to build some closeness and confidence in our gun section. That was a very different approach to how Sergeant Likens had run his section, keeping us in a separate tent from him and the two corporals. I told the section each day at 1600 hours, "Let's go get our two beers!" We built up some "*esprit de corps*" pretty quickly in this gun section at Phu Bai.

One of our section, Ken Anderson, told me that he knew where there was a bunch of leftover lumber stacked up. He came up with this idea for designing a fancy crew bunker for us. A metal ammunition pallet fits perfectly for a floor. Once we got started, it didn't take long to finish. I got permission not to send any of the gun section on work parties and patrols during the bunker's construction.

Chapter 21

Vietcong Mortar Rounds

The full battery position at Phu Bai was set up in a circle of four acres. The layout was reminiscent of a circle of wagons that you would see in the old cowboy movies that we used to watch. This gave us a small fortified area, but close fighting seemed to work well when we had so few Marines to defend the battery position. The gun pits for three M53 155mm guns and three M55 8-inch howitzers made up the northern half of the camp area. The southern half consisted of headquarters bunkers, the motor transportation pool, communications bunkers, our FDC bunker, and areas for the maintenance, staff NCOs and officers bunkers. Eighty to a hundred Marines and three Navy corpsmen were on strength with the 1st 155mm Gun Battery at Phu Bai in January 1967.

We laughed about it quite a bit for all of the chaos it caused, but officers and staff non-commissioned officers and just about every rank and MOS were constantly coming and going from the 1st Guns. I'm sure it was a nightmare for First Lieutenant Upton and First Lieutenant Day, the two officers in charge in between commanding officers coming and going. We would get a captain for a commanding officer, and he would leave. Then a major showed up, and then he left, then another captain, and then he left. Lieutenant Day always took over as the Commanding Officer.

I was given the job of making sure that all the machine guns were set up around the perimeter. There were about twelve of them, .50 caliber M2s and 7.62mm M-60s. All were set up around the battery so they had a good field of fire and plenty of ammunition. I also checked each one so that we were not shooting into the backs of our outer positions. The main thing machine gunners watched out for were flashes from enemy mortar tubes. You could easily see someone light a match 200 yards away at night because it got so dark.

On 21 January,1967, VC mortar rounds were fired at us, exploding behind our battery. There was a Seabee base there called Camp Campbell a few hundred yards behind us. I quickly got on the landline telephone and listened in on the conversation between the FDC bunker and the outposts. We fired on the mortar flashes with machine guns and were ordered to cease fire. "What?" I wondered – why would we cease fire? All the Marines in the 1st Guns were really upset about the cease fire order, but there was a reason. The Viet Cong had set up their mortars between us and the nearby village, which was a designated no fire zone. The Viet Cong continued to fire their mortars after our battery stopped firing the machine guns. The After Action Report typed up in the aftermath of the attack told a grim tale.

> At approximately 0145 on 21 January 1967, Camp Campbell received six rounds of 82mm mortar fire. This was a portion of the total of fifty-nine rounds taken within the Phu Bai Combat Base. One hit in the Alpha Company berthing area and one in the Delta Company area sustained direct hits. Francis Camden (Equipment Operator Third Class (E03)) and Merlin Boon were killed, and seventeen Seabees were wounded.

The next morning, I drove a first sergeant over to the Seabee base and we saw the damage, all the parts of their camp which was destroyed just five hours earlier. We talked to a Navy Chief Petty Officer (E-7), and he talked to us about the injuries and deaths. Later I saw the After-Action Report stating that two sailors had been killed and seventeen had been wounded. The first sergeant didn't tell the Navy Chief we were given a cease fire order during the mortar attack.

The mortar rounds just kept on falling. We had a good view from on top of our ammunition bunker and we watched the mortar barrels flash and the mortars bombs impacting. I have always thought those VC mortar rounds were aimed at our battery. After all, why would the Viet Cong waste all those mortar rounds firing on the Seabee compound with an artillery battery right next door? In 2015, almost fifty years later, I met Seabee Ron Bowen who was at Camp Campbell on the night of the mortar attack. He escorted the body of Merlin Boon home to Oklahoma for burial. We talked on the telephone for a long time. He sent some pictures to me.

Above and below: The mortar damage at Camp Campbell, Phu Bai, in January 1967.

The very next day at our battery's enlisted men's club, everyone began talking about writing to their congressmen. It was hard to believe we received a cease fire order when our comrades were under fire. Within a week at morning formation, we were told to stop writing to our congressmen. Somebody yelled, "I'll write to whoever I want to write to." Nothing more was said about that and we were all dismissed. As I was walking away, a first sergeant walked over to me and remarked; "Hilton – you had better get your gun section under control." I said, "They'll be fine, Sergeant."

Chapter 22

Heating Our Tent

While standing on watch it was always hard to stay dry. We were burning blocks of C4 explosives to heat our tent and to dry out our boots, socks, and utilities. To this day, I'm convinced we were killing ourselves with that C4, because it had to be putting off toxic fumes as it burned. A maintenance truck pulled up to the gun pit entrance and they gave us a heater and a 55-gallon drum of diesel fuel. The maintenance guys helped us assemble and connect it and showed us how to get that new stove going. The maintenance guys asked us if there was a vent in our tent for the heater. "Well, it's a brand-new tent, we just have to look up under that flap on top."

Sure enough, the Navy Seabees tent had a metal vent built into that new canvas tent that we had "borrowed" from them. Everyone pitched in and we had that heater set up and working and heating the tent in a short time. Sometimes the fire went out, but we had plenty of gasoline to get it going again. Diesel is hard to get started so we used gasoline. What could be better than to keep an open bucket of gasoline right next to a heater of burning fire?

One night I had just finished a couple of hours of rainy guard duty watching the gun, it was midnight, and I was soaking wet. The crew was sleeping, and the fire had gone out in the heater. I opened the top lid to the heater and picked up the "milk bucket" that was about half full of gasoline and poured just a little gasoline on the top of the soot in the bottom of the heater. I could not see any fire because of the black soot covering the bottom. But the fire was there, and that gasoline found it.

In an instant the whole bucket of gasoline caught fire. I panicked and dropped it, but it didn't tip over, it hit the wood floor on its bottom and splashed fire right over on one sleeping Marine's head. His whole head was on fire as he jumped up yelling and ran across the floor only to land on top of another sleeping Marine. That Marine woke up with this guy on fire screaming and he started screaming. The whole crew awoke, and I watched all this in complete shock. The tent floor was on fire and the half bucket of gasoline was burning like wildfire. The Marine on the bottom quickly covered the burning head of the Marine on fire with a blanket. I then grabbed another blanket and tossed it towards the fire on the floor and bucket. The blanket spread out and smothered the fire, and just like that it was put out immediately. It was a miracle. The unfortunate Marine who's head caught fire lost all of his hair, his eyebrows, and eyelashes. The panicked look on the poor guy's face was enough to make anyone feel sick, but the look of his burnt off hair was even more shocking. He was all right, and would survive, but all his hair was gone. It was one of the strangest things I had ever seen.

There was complete silence in the aftermath, and then someone asked, "Who in the hell started that damn fire?"

I was the only one standing, and so I said, "I did – and it's not a good idea to have that gasoline so close to the stove."

We all started laughing and we laughed all night long. We laughed for days after that about the fire. We also found a smaller container for storing

The type of heater we used for the tent.

our gasoline. In the following days the Marine who was set on fire and the Marine who put the fire out both left the gun section. These marines were just passing through and waiting for new orders. We never saw them again.

All through February I had trained the section, and I could tell that the gun section wanted to get involved in combat. They wanted to do something more meaningful than just filling sandbags, going out on work parties, and "burning the crapper". The guys in the section wanted to kill Viet Cong. They wanted to see some action, and I guess everybody did when they first got there. Marines are trained to carry a rifle, and to kill. They want to be tested and they want to be in combat. They want to know what they are made of. A friend told me he went through twelve weeks of Marine Corps boot camp, and two weeks of Infantry training and was handed a typewriter. He felt that was a terrible let-down. He spent four years typing reports and keeping records on the Marines in the field.

Chapter 23

First Operation for Gun Six

One morning in March after the morning formation, Lieutenant Day told me that my M53 Gun and an M55 8-inch howitzer had been chosen to participate in a joint operation. We would be under the operational control of the 12th Marines and the Army of the Republic of Vietnam (ARVN). This was a bad idea right from the start. I didn't trust the ARVN. Many ARVN soldiers were not interested in fighting for their government, and some had family with communist sympathies. We couldn't tell if some of them sympathized with the Viet Cong.

Lieutenant Day ordered us to pack up our gear and drive the M53 north on Highway 1, and to turn west at the PK-17 mile marker. We would then reach the base camp of the headquarters, 12th Marine Regiment north of Hue City. The 12th Marines were the artillery regiment attached to the 3rd Marine Division and it was made up of four artillery battalions. These included the 1st, 2nd and 3rd Battalions, all equipped with M101A1 105mm howitzers, and the 4th battalion, which was equipped with M114A1 155mm howitzers for most of its batteries, but also included a battery of very modern M109 self-propelled howitzers. PK-17 itself was an ARVN compound seventeen kilometers north of Hue City. PK stood for "*poste kilometres*". The French had marked everything in kilometers when they administered Vietnam as part of their colony of *Indochine* many years earlier. We would be moving closer to the DMZ, which ran along the border between north and south Vietnam. (Note: PK-17 and Gia Le are both mentioned in *Hue 1968* by Mark Bowden).

The gun section was excited about leaving on the operation, and especially about getting away from the staff NCOs and officers. They all wanted an adventure outside the battery compound in Phu Bai. I told the men to start packing ammunition and powder in our 5-ton truck and its trailer. We packed up our belongings and placed them on top of the ammunition and powder. The last thing we would pack would be the tent. It would have to come down, and we would stow it on top of our personal belongings. We also had to bring empty sandbags, rolls of barbed wire, and lots of fence posts. There was a lot of work involved to move a 155mm gun!

I told the driver to start the M53's engine up and to drive it off the big recoil spade that it sits on when in firing positions. I locked that huge 155mm gun barrel in its clamp for road travel. Disaster struck next. The driver yelled over to me that while the M53's engine would start up, he could not get the transmission into gear. The engine ran, but the M53 would not move. I called for the battery's mechanics, and they got to work, but no matter what they did, nobody could get that gun to move. It could fire, but could not move. So, in the end we didn't get to go north on that operation to PK-17 with the 12th Marines. We stayed in the perimeter and fired support missions for the Marine RECON teams in the field. The whole business was very disappointing for the gun section.

Another M53 155mm gun and crew were chosen for the operation and they duly packed up and headed up north on Highway 1. Just south of Hue City the M53 broke down. It took all day for a big M51 recovery tractor to arrive and haul it back to a repair facility over by the Phu Bai airport. We were down another gun. Lieutenant Day decided to send two M55 8-inch howitzers to PK-17 to make up the numbers. With the other M53 155mm gun over in the repair shop, it just gave us more targets to shoot at with our own gun. We kept ourselves busy shooting as fire missions were called in, and with finishing off the construction of our big ammunition bunker.

M51 Tow Tractor to haul M53 155mm guns. (From 1ˢᵗ 155mm Guns)

Chapter 24

Two New Sergeants

One day when I was walking over to the FDC bunker, a staff sergeant introduced me to a newly arrived sergeant. He was a very weathered looking Marine. The staff sergeant said the new sergeant was not going to be my gun's section chief, but he was being assigned my gun. The new sergeant was not a trained artilleryman, and we'd have to show him the job. I walked the new sergeant back to our gun and introduced him to all the guys in the section. Then I showed him the ammunition bunker, and how the ammunition was stored inside the bunker. I asked him if he had a problem hauling ammunition when we had a fire mission. "No problem" was his reply.

I told the new sergeant that if he heard "GUN SIX FIRE MISSION!" yelled across the battery, he had to come running. "I don't care if you're in the crapper, or having a drink in the club, just drop what you're doing and run over to the gun." The sergeant understood these instructions. He just had one question: "When did the club open?"

Shortly after the new sergeant arrived, Lieutenant Day took me aside. He told me that another sergeant had arrived, and that he would be taking over Gun Six as the Section Chief. I felt like I had just been gut-punched. I guess my feelings were hurt. I was already very close to the gun crew. We had built closeness with one another

Sergeant Bradish.

by completing tasks together, and I didn't want to lose that. I was planning on making sergeant (E-5) because Section Chiefs were sergeants and staff sergeants. Lieutenant Day could see that I was upset.

"Now listen Hilton, a corporal cannot be in charge of two sergeants…" he said. As we were walking over to the mess hall, he said he had other duties for me to do. He introduced me to Sergeant Bradish, a young-looking Marine who was already on his second tour in Vietnam. His first tour was in mortars. We sat and we talked, and I gave him the short run down about our M53 gun and our crew. He said as soon as they promoted him to sergeant in the States, they sent him back to Vietnam. I felt sorry for him, because nobody likes being the new guy.

I took Sergeant Bradish over to our gun and introduced him to the crew. I told the gun section that Bradish was going to be the new Section Chief. The men of the gun crew were kind of quiet. We still had plenty of room in our tent and I asked Bradish where he wanted to sleep. He said he wanted his own tent to sleep in, separate from the crew. I said that was fine, the other sergeant could go with him too. We set up a two-man canvas tent for the sergeants, right beside our new tent.

Chapter 25

Corporal Gopher

I became corporal "Gopher". My new duties from Lieutenant Day were to go for this, go for that. It made the days in Vietnam go fast. I decided I'd just stay busy and focus on 15 July, the day I was scheduled to go home. We were getting a pretty good stream of new Marines in the battery in that period. Lieutenant Day gave me the job of taking the new arrivals out to an open area to test fire their rifles and sight them in. I let them shoot our M60 and M2 .50 caliber machine guns. I gave them boxes of ammunition to shoot, in fact hundreds of rounds. Then I would inspect them as they cleaned the machine guns. I had already learnt that the hands-on approach was the best way to learn about weapons.

I got other assignments too. If a Section Chief left on R&R for a week, I took over that section and ran the gun in his absence. I also drove staff NCOs and new lieutenants around from time to time. In those instances I was not just their driver, but also their bodyguard. I still did my share of guard duty, but on a more favorable schedule than most of the others.

I stayed on the M53 and took the first gun watch in the evening for two hours each night. After that I could sleep until 0500 hours. I also helped on the Reactionary Force. That was where eight Marines slept together with weapons and ammunition within easy reach. The Reactionary Force was formed each night, in case the battery was attacked. It was our task to reinforce any part of the camp perimeter or to help out the ammo handling on any gun section if and emergency fire mission was called in. That Reaction Force was somebody's great idea!

On 5 April 1967 I had to drive a new second lieutenant up to PK-17 so he could meet Lieutenant Upton (who was the officer in charge of two M55 8-inch howitzers). A Jeep was prepared with sandbags on both floorboards,

I still had to help out with Fire Missions and cleaning the M53's 155mm tube. It always took four or five Marines to swab that long tube out.

and across the front of the windshield just in case we ran over a landmine – or were shot at by a sniper. When I picked the lieutenant up, he looked a little surprised with all the sandbags stacked and piled. I said: "Welcome to the Nam, Lieutenant".

Now I hadn't seen my friend John Brophy for several weeks. I was looking forward to seeing John and several of the other guys serving on the howitzers. The second lieutenant and I were to drive to the Phu Bai airport, join a convoy and travel north. In Vietnam we Marines called our armed convoys "rough riders". There was every type of military vehicle you could think of in these convoys. There were 5-ton and 10-ton trucks full of troops or pulling artillery, loaded ammunition trucks pulling trailers, tanks, dusters, jeeps – a whole mass of military personnel and equipment all armed to the teeth and going north.

I was accustomed to speeding up and down Highway 1 in 5-ton trucks on ammo runs. We would drive as fast as those trucks could go. We had never gone far as part of a rough rider. Things had already changed in the Phu Bai area since my arrival in Vietnam. By April 1967 a drive to Hue City was not as safe as it had been in 1966. Rough rider convoys were very slow, and driving wasn't easy because the USMC trucks were not fitted with brake lights. I almost slammed into the back of a 5-ton truck ahead of us twice. The new lieutenant never said a word, but if looks could kill, I would have been one dead Marine. With so many sandbags on the floor, I could not brake easily. I stopped the jeep in the middle of the road and pulled one sandbag out and just threw it out onto the road. I thought it was kind of funny. I kept driving, but the lieutenant did not talk. It was going to be a long ride to PK-17.

That rough rider kept stopping, because it was getting held up by landmines. An engineer had to check for explosives under every bridge that we came upon. We were already getting some sniper fire from a group of trees. While we waited for that sniper to be cleared, one of our jets came in and dropped a canister of napalm. It landed really close to us, and as it exploded; I felt the strangest sensation. Everything moved in slow motion for me, including the jet. That jet kind of hung in mid-air. I could feel the heat of the napalm, and just that fast, everything was back in real time. The lieutenant never said a word.

After a long, slow drive we finally turned west onto the dirt road off Highway 1. We saw our battery's two 8-inch howitzers in their positions. I pointed to the FDC van and told the second lieutenant that Lieutenant Upton would be in there. I told the officer that I'd leave the jeep by the FDC and would come for him later to catch the rough rider back south to Phu Bai. The officer and I went our separate ways, and I found my friend John Brophy. He told me I'd arrived just in time for lunch. John gave me a tray and a spoon, and we walked over to the small mess hall. Lieutenant Upton's detachment were feeding several other Marines from other outfits. There was no place to sit, everyone just stood out in the hot sun at a long counter made from plywood. We'd eat and then we'd move on.

John and I walked around the compound, but I was shocked by what I saw. Some whitewashed buildings were very close to the two M55s. "What are those buildings for?" I asked. John said "that's where the ARVN soldiers sleep". The two 8-inch howitzers were side by side, facing in opposite directions. One M55 faced north, and the other faced south. The back of one howitzer was exposed to an open area. There was no protection for that crew at all. I said I'd never seen any artillery set up like this before. John said they had only just set those guns up this morning. There was hardly any wire strung around the compound, and there was none between the howitzers and the ARVN compound. One hundred 8-inch high explosive rounds were sitting out in the open, not in a bunker.

Ammunition bunker. (Picture from 1st 155mm Guns web page)

Lieutenant Upton's detachment at PK-17 had two Army 40mm M42 Dusters attached. Those tracks were intended to help with perimeter security around two M55 howitzers, but for the moment they seemed to be parked outside the compound. Me and John both just shook our heads when we saw that. The detachment just didn't have enough Marines available on these operations to set up a proper wire compound to protect the howitzers or their gun sections. I thought that if the enemy attacked, the sappers were going to come from those white buildings and easily overrun the M55s and the whole of PK-17. It was good to visit with John and to catch up with several of the others from our battery, but I had a bad feeling about PK-17. A very uneasy feeling.

"Hilton!" yelled the second lieutenant. "We have to go." I jumped in the Jeep and we drove off to catch that rough rider heading back south to Phu Bai. We got to a closed gate guarded by Marines with machine guns, still on PK-17. A sergeant told us we had missed the rough rider. The second lieutenant insisted: "I have orders, so open that gate." The sergeant looked at me and said, "when you get to Highway 1 and if you can't see that rough rider, just turn around and come back." I saw two young Marines standing with a huge sea-bag. I asked them what they were doing. Once they announced that they had also missed the rough rider, I told them to get in. I thought two more Marines with rifles in our Jeep would be a big help to us if we needed more fire power. The second lieutenant had only come armed with a 45-caliber pistol.

The two Marines piled into the small area in the back of the jeep along with the sea-bag. We drove away very quickly. When we got to Highway 1, I stopped. It was very quiet, kind of scary even. The lieutenant shouted "Go!" so I floored the jeep's accelerator. We were flying down Highway 1 and there was no sign of the rough rider. We drove up a small hill, but there was still no sign of any vehicles. Suddenly I saw a broken-down Vietnamese bus. I slammed the brakes on – this could be an ambush. I told the lieutenant to pull out his pistol, but he didn't. I told the Marines in the back to stick their rifles out the sides. They did. I also put my M-14 across my lap and floored the jeep. We must have gone by that broken down bus full of people at 70 miles per hour. They must have thought we were crazy Marines. We drove hell for leather around turns, and over hills and then we finally saw a vehicle. It was the rough riders' last security jeep. The driver waved for me to get in front of him and we drove on south to Phu Bai. When we finally arrived at Phu Bai I dropped off the two Marines. To this day I wonder what they had in that sea-bag. As for the second lieutenant, after we got back to our battery, he never asked me to drive him anywhere again.

Chapter 26

PK-17 Overrun

Our detachment at PK-17 was mortared and overrun by sappers on 6 April 1967 – the morning after we had left. The USMC after action report which followed the ordeal of its defenders stated that one of our battery's Navy corpsmen was wounded, the other Corpsmen "Doc" Himmerick, and Marine Ernie Gutierrez were killed. Two other Marines from the 4th Battalion, 12th Marines were killed alongside them. This was such sad news. Ernie Gutierrez, a Mexican American from San Jose, California, was

Above left: Ernie Gutierrez.

Above right: Doc Himmerick, USN.

in his 13th month in Vietnam and had just seven days left until he was due to go home. He would have turned 20 on 15 April, and had been telling people that there was going to be a big party when he got home on his birthday. What a shame he never made it. Before he died he had given a ring to another Marine for safekeeping and asked that it be given to his mother if anything should happen to him. Many years later I talked to Gutierrez's nephew, who remembered his mother (Ernie's sister) mentioning a Marine who came to their house to give the family Ernie's ring. He told me that the family had been planning a big welcome home and birthday party for him, but the bad news came and the party never happened.

Michael Himmerick was a native of Valley City, North Dakota. He had volunteered for the United States Navy to see the world. The Navy had made him a corpsman and he was sent to the 3rd Marine Division and took his place with the 1st 155mm Gun Battery (Self-Propelled). A few months earlier I had been given an injection by "Doc" Himmerick. I had walked into the small two-man tent and asked him if he wanted to inject my arm with the Marine Corps tattoo or the other arm. Doc didn't reply – he was too busy mixing the medicine for my injection. I looked around his tent and I saw a loaded .45 caliber pistol and his cartridge belt hanging on a tent pole, along with his medical bag. His helmet and flak jacket were at the foot of his rack. Doc Himmerick looked more like a Marine, than a sailor. "Corporal Hilton," he said, "that tattoo would make a nice target, but this shot is going a little lower. Turn around and pull your pants down … and this is going to hurt."

The Doc had a sense of humor. Once after a morning formation he yelled out to the company commander (a captain) and waved the needle and syringe in the air. The captain just walked over to Doc and pulled down his pants in front of all of us young Marines to get his shot. It wasn't a pretty sight, but it sure was funny. Doc's mother, father and one brother have long since passed away. He also had a sister, and her two daughters have contacted me. The two nieces had never met Doc because they hadn't been born when he was sent to Vietnam. I only knew him as "Doc Himmerick", and didn't even know that his first name was Michael. His family called him Mickey.

The two Marines from the 4/12th were both men we were familiar with – so much so that I thought they were members of our own battery. Sergeant Jack Duff was one of these men, I found out from talking to his three sisters and his brother years later that he was from the motor transportation platoon with the 4/12th Marines. One of his sisters and I have become friends on Facebook, and we still text occasionally. I never knew Lance Corporal Fredsti. I later saw a tribute on one of the Vietnam websites which mentioned his name, with a woman asking if anybody knew about him. I tried to contact her, but she never wrote back.

During the attack on PK-17, one of the M55 8-inch howitzers had fired directly into the complex of white buildings from which the enemy sappers had attacked the position. The shells had utterly destroyed those buildings, and the twenty dead enemy sappers slain in the attack were later buried in PK-17's soft sand. Then our Marines placed four rifles muzzle down in the sand, to commemorate our four fallen comrades. We later held a memorial

FROM MARINE CORPS RECORDS: "AFTER ACTION REPORT".

The 1st 155mm Gun and 8" Howitzer Battery was assigned to the 4th Bn, 12th Marines. In early April 1967 its 8" Howitzer and 155mm Gun Platoon was based at PK-17, a joint USMC-ARVN camp a few miles north of Hue. The 1st 155th's Command Chronology for April 1967 contains the following entry:

"In the early hours of 6 April, 2 Companies of the 800th [NVA] Battalion along with the C112 Sapper Unit attacked the ARVN & USMC camp at PK 17 (YD647277) with a mortar and ground attack. After overrunning the ARVN portion of the camp, the Viet Cong turned on the 8" Howitzer and 155mm Gun Platoon. Using small arms, automatic weapons, grenades and the direct fire of the 8" howitzer and the 155mm Gun, the Marines held the perimeter for three hours before the VC withdrew. The platoon lost 1 USMC KIA, 1 USN KIA, 8 USMC WIA and one 8" Howitzer out of action due to a direct hit with a mortar round. The enemy losses were 20 KIA ! (confirmed) inside the compound and 40 KIA (probable)."
Two men were killed outright in the attack and two of the wounded died over the next few days:

Sgt Jack C. Duff, Kansas City, MO (DoW 04/07/1967)
LCpl Steffan M. Fredsti, Simi, CA (DoW 04/14/1967)
LCpl Ernest L. Gutierrez, San Jose, CA.
HN Michael D. Himmerick, Valley City, ND.

A tribute I have posted on Memorial Day several times over the years.

PK-17: You can see the ARVN sleeping quarters in the white buildings in the background. Notice, no wire or protection from the ARVN and the Marines' position. The sappers attacked from those buildings. (Picture of PK 17 from the 1st 155mm Guns web page)

service for the three Marines and for Doc Himmerick at Phu Bai. It was a moving experience and all I remember of it was looking down in the white sand where I stood as the battery commander spoke. I could not tell you what he said, for all I could think about was the loss their families would feel. What was Ernie Gutierrez's mother going to say when she got news that her son had been killed days before his birthday? I felt like crying. Our detachment at PK-17 was now three men down. After the service, Sergeant Bradish (who was the new section chief on my M53) volunteered to go north to make up the numbers in the M55 detachment. He was accompanied by Ken Anderson and Jerry Hunt. I stayed in Phu Bai with our M53 gun and the rest of the gun section. That very night PK-17 was mortared again, but there was no ground attack from the sappers like the previous night.

We were informed that we were not just fighting the VC anymore, and that the enemy now included regular troops from the North Vietnamese Army. I had been in the Marines for twenty months, and in Vietnam for eleven months. We were told that an NVA battalion consisted of 400 to 500 soldiers, regular infantry which usually included sappers. The Viet Cong were guerillas. Up to that time I had never heard anything about fighting NVA soldiers, just about Viet Cong. I talked to plenty of other Marines who had never heard of the NVA either. Some said they had seen them in the distance along the DMZ and had just let them walk on by. One Marine said he had waved to them up there, and they waved back. It is a crazy thing in war, but when people are not told who they are supposed to fight, things like this could easily happen. We certainly knew we'd be fighting NVA from that time onwards. The whole thing confused me. Up until that time – April 1967 – I was focused entirely on Viet Cong. In boot camp it had all been "VC this, VC that". Never was anything once said about North Vietnam even having an army. The Marines were given I-Corps with the express mission to kill Viet Cong. We had never heard anything about killing any NVA soldiers.

Chapter 27

Phu Bai Combat Base Under Attack

On the night of 27/28 April 1967 I was detailed to the rapid reaction force. We always kept eight Marines in the rapid reaction force (usually one from each gun section), and the rest of the numbers were made up from whoever was available in the battery. The rapid reaction force slept in one tent with weapons handy, just in case the battery was ever attacked. The rapid reaction force tent was situated close to the FDC bunker. If the perimeter was attacked the officers and staff NCOs from the FDC could direct us to resupply the Marines in the perimeter bunkers with ammunition or help with ammunition handling on any M53 or M55 given a fire mission. I thought it was a good idea having this rapid reaction force to hold our perimeter, especially after what had taken place at PK-17. Being in the rapid reaction force was a good job. We'd report in around 1800 hours and then go watch a movie, or just kick back and write letters. If nothing much happened, we might even get a good night's sleep.

As I was lying there on my cot, I started to have second thoughts about this war. The battery's first gun crews had all rotated home and the battery had received so many new Marines. Then there was the needless tragedy of PK-17 with Ernie and Doc Himmerick both being killed and others wounded. One M55 8-inch howitzer had been put out of commission. I remembered driving that lieutenant north to PK-17. I thought of the jet dropping napalm close to Highway 1. The little finger on my left hand had been shaking some, a nervous twitch that I'd never had before. It all seemed kind of strange. And I was tired, really tired. I had seventy-five days left on my tour, seventy-five days until I could leave this place. My mind raced, but I was exhausted, and I fell into a deep sleep.

Next thing I knew, I was awake. Not to the crash of enemy mortar rounds blowing up outside our tent – but to the sound of the Marine next to me slamming his foot into his boot on the wooden floor of the tent. I sat up quickly and asked "what's happening?"

The Marine yelled in reply, "We are getting hit!"

All eight of us quickly got up and grabbed our rifles, helmets, 782 gear and flak jackets. We ran to the FDC bunker to see if they needed us to go to the outer perimeter. A new sergeant who had been taking patrols out during the day said, "we are going out there." With all the machine guns firing, I quickly said "that's a bad idea, sergeant." A lieutenant came out of the FDC bunker and yelled, "get in that bunker." I was standing at the entrance of a very small, sandbagged bunker. I had never seen any fighting positions like this. It even had a roof on it.

I quickly went down into the bunker and the other seven Marines followed me. As they piled in they smashed me up against the sandbagged wall at the end of the bunker. I could see a small loophole to look out of and to place my rifle through. My rifle was in a vertical position and with everyone packed in that bunker; I could not point my rifle through that opening. I have never been claustrophobic, but this time I felt real panic. I remember praying that God would get me out of that bunker. I finally pushed and crawled out and just sat beside the back of it, guarding the entrance to the FDC bunker. I figured if the Sappers were going to overrun

The morning formation. Also, the small bunker that I was in during the 28 April 1967, attack. (Courtesy Bob Simington)

141

These are the regular fighting positions. No roofs, just sandbags.

this battery, like they had at PK-17, this FDC bunker would be a target because all the officers and staff NCOs were inside.

Our machine guns were firing on the west side of the battery perimeter, and our 155mm guns across from us were firing directly out into their field of fire. Illumination flares were going up all over the place, lighting up the night just like a Friday night high-school football game. The battle was described in our battery's after-action report pretty much as I have paraphrased below:

> At 0130 on 28 April the Phu Bai combat base came under mortar attack. An outpost spotted the flashes, and the battery was the first in the Phu Bai Perimeter to take the enemy under attack, fixing them with .50 caliber machine guns and with the attached Army M42 40mm self-propelled AA guns. During this time the battery fired counter-rocket fire plans as directed by 3rd BN, 26th Marines. 7 enemy soldiers were killed. A morning patrol revealed the battery counter-mortar fire netted 70 enemy killed in action. The battery suffered two minor wounded in action.

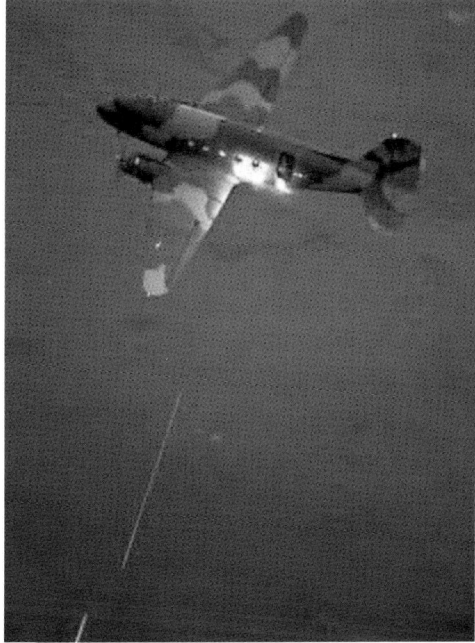

Right and below: AC47 Shooting down at the enemy. (Courtesy of Donald Luke, Crew Chief of a Spooky AC47 Gunship. Web page www.ac 47-gunships.com)

The US Air Force made its appearance too. Spooky the AC-47 gunship was called in, and it made several passes around the perimeter. Its machine guns sprayed thousands of rounds of 7.62mm fire into the enemy's positions. The rate of fire from its miniguns was so heavy that in the dark it looked like red ropes were being dropped out of the side of that AC-47. The sound it made was also pretty unique compared to a normal machine gun, almost like a burping noise. "BURRRRRRRRRRP". It was a sight to behold!

A nearby 105mm howitzer battery had our range and we soon saw the friendly shells falling around our perimeter. My M53's section loaded 20-pound powder charge bags without projectiles and fired them as is, which fired the exploding charge bags into the enemy positions in huge fireballs. No ceasefire was given this night, and we kept firing until dawn. Then there was silence. The seventy enemy dead were dragged into two separate swallow graves, confirmed by our Navy corpsman and one of our corporals. The NVA had probably dragged as many wounded and dead with them as they could, so the number of enemy casualties was probably higher.

Chapter 28

No Man's Land

A day later I was detailed to man a perimeter outpost between our battery position and an adjacent Marine unit. I called it "no man's land". The men from our battery had been running wire in that area for a long time, but the other Marine unit still has not taken it under their control. We were guarding that area because it seemed a likely point for another enemy attack. The three of us brought our M-14 rifles and we had an M-60 machine gun. No landline phone line was set up out there. We were just on our own, and we had to be vigilant. We were given a case of C-Rations and we enjoyed eating them. The other two Marines came from other parts of the battery, one from the FDC and the other from the motor transportation platoon. None of us knew each other, but my two colleagues found out while talking that they were from the same city. Those two became best friends, but I just wanted to get back to my gun section.

My two colleagues offered to take over the midnight to 0600 hours watch if I let them go to a movie back in the battery. Usually, the movies were from a series called "Combat" starring Vic Morrow. I told them that would be fine, so they went and then came back to the outpost. It was a really dark night in Phu Bai. Soon after they returned, we saw a light shining out in the area in front of us. It was somebody with an old gas lantern walking across our frontage about a hundred yards away. One of my colleagues asked if he could shoot the guy. I told him to wait to see if the lantern bearer turned and came towards us.

Just then, the light stopped, and then it started coming towards us. The Viet Cong were known for putting a lantern on a long bamboo pole and walking to the side of it while coming towards you in order to draw fire. When they got close, they would engage with a hand grenade, with rifle fire, or even with an RPG. Who knew what weapons they could have? I had heard that sometimes they would use a woman with a couple of children to hide their presence. Sometimes those women had weapons too. I told the Marine to fire. He fired and hit the lantern. There was a big flash of fire when he hit it. My first thoughts were to congratulate him for good shooting. Nothing else happened over the next hour.

When the clock struck midnight the two Marines were still talking about the good old days back home – who they knew and what schools they went to, and so on. I said good night to them and laid out my canvas shelter half and rolled up in it, because it started to rain very hard. Those two Marines had the watch for the next six hours. When I woke up at 0600, we walked out front of our position about a hundred yards out to see if there was a dead Viet Cong. We could not find anyone. When I looked back at the outpost I saw Lieutenant Day standing there by himself, hands on hips. I told the two Marines that we are probably in trouble for not cleaning up those C-Rations. I then said, "Let's walk around the outside perimeter to the front gate, and then go our separate ways."

I was right about getting into trouble, and it wasn't long before my name was called to go and see Lieutenant Day. As I stood in front of him at attention before his desk, he said that he'd been about to promote me to sergeant E-5, but firing my weapon without permission was against the rules (because I was in charge of the two other Marines and allowed one to fire his rifle without permission from an officer, I was held accountable for the shooting). I told him about the lantern we'd seen, and that as we lacked any means of communication with the FDC Bunker, it had been an executive decision. There was no telephone line run out to that outpost. Lieutenant Day didn't care, as far as he was concerned rules were rules. He said he would not give me what they called "office hours", meaning his reservations were not written in my records, "but you will not make sergeant E-5 here in Vietnam. You'll be promoted to sergeant back in the States once you go home. You are dismissed!"

It was a confusing maze of getting permissions and no-nos for a junior NCO in the Marines, and I was bitter about it. There were the free-fire zones, the no-fire zones and we had to ask for permission to shoot a rifle; there were more inspections and we'd been told to start polishing our boots in country. We'd also just been told we couldn't go without T-shirts unless we were in our own areas. The growth of the huge list of Marine Corps craziness amid a real war just continued.

It was a paradox because the USMC also got lax on disciplinary issues elsewhere. The officers had lifted the restriction on only two beers a day and they now let the enlisted Marines drink all the beer they wanted. I saw loads of drunken Marines and I didn't think that was a good thing. I often saw Marines throwing up because they'd drunk too much beer. Several Marines had dropped artillery rounds on their feet and toes while hungover and were sent to see a corpsman. One Marine in my gun section caught part of his finger in the M53's 155mm gun breach as it was being closed, and he'd been cut badly. I wrapped his cut finger with a dirty rag and sent him off to see a corpsman. All those Marines received Purple Hearts.

Beer was not the only problem. Marijuana use had begun to spread across the battery as well. The Vietnamese called marijuana joints "crazy cigarettes". You could buy them anywhere in Vietnam. I tried marijuana myself around that time but, apart from the fact that it made me paranoid, I knew I was supposed to be an example to my juniors, so I didn't repeat the experience. The officers and staff NCOs did not even know about marijuana smoking in the junior ranks.

To be honest, the 1st 155mm Gun Battery was a different battery by May 1967 from when I had first arrived in back in June 1966. We didn't have to ask for permission to fire our weapon. The Marines in the outpost next to mine even threw a hand grenade in the middle of the night when they thought they'd heard something close by. Nobody questioned them. We could go without T-shirts, and nobody shined their boots. I cannot remember any inspections after that either.

Chapter 29

Mess Duty

During that May of 1967 someone had to do mess duty for thirty days from our Gun section, a job nobody wanted. I volunteered for it, because it was better for me to do it than a Marine from the gun section. We're getting new Marines in, and they need to learn the 155mm Gun and ammunition. When I reported at the mess hall and first saw the cook, a sergeant, he told me he didn't need another cook. I saw a stack of dirty pots and pans and told him I'd just wash up. The cook was happy with that. I used to work in three different bakeries as a teenager and it was some hard work cleaning up

I'm on the left helping mix the Kool-Aid in the drinking water.

Mess duty for thirty days at Phu Bai. Notice the 50-foot tower in the background.

At Phu Bai we employed a 50-foot tower for observation. The Seabees built it for us, and one day I climbed to the top of the tower, just to say I had been up there. The Marines on the guns didn't have to guard up there. The Fire Direction Center (FDC) Marines manned that tower 24/7. When we went on patrol, if we found "Mortar Base Plate" marks in the sand near our perimeter, we called back to the tower by radio and the FDC Marines marked that position. Fifty years later I found out that the Seabees had built five of those towers around the south and western side of Phu Bai. Ours was the first one to be built.

after those bakers. This was easy work and I kept myself busy and helped wherever I could.

I also helped setting up the cans of hot water to clean the cooking utensils. That part of the job was a real pain, but it made the days go by fast. I woke at 0500 and started helping to get the mess hall set up for breakfast. The cook prepared two meals a day. Because I could drive a truck, the cook sent me to get food from the refrigerated warehouse next to the Phu Bai airport. It was just a few miles away. According to the cook they even kept milk over there. Milk was something I had not tasted once since I had left the United States eleven months previously.

I drove a truck over to the refrigerated warehouse and once I arrived a sergeant told me where the milk was. I walked up to what I thought was a refrigerated container, but to my horror I discovered it was a freezer. A freezer full of body bags. I was shocked. In fact I was just about frozen in total shock, and I forgot about the milk. It hurt me deep inside, and it still hurts me to this day when I recall those stacked body bags filled with the remains of our Marines. I have never forgotten that sight. Years later, one of the men who had been assigned to casualty collection explained to me how our dead were sent home. Normally when a soldier was KIA on the battlefield his unit collected his weapon and ammunition before the body was placed in a body bag. All of his personal belongings like rings or a wallet, and his IDs, were left with the remains for transfer to an established collection point.

Collection points were distributed throughout South Vietnam and they were normally manned by personnel trained in mortuary affairs. An initial attempt at identification was made at the collection point where a "toe-tag" was attached to the remains with a "believe-to-be (BTB)" name carefully noted. Once this had been done, the remains were then transported to the nearest mortuary.

The United States had two mortuaries in Vietnam; one in Da Nang; and a second in Saigon. These two mortuaries took care of all American KIAs from all branches of service as well as any KIAs from free-world Allied forces (i.e. Canadians serving in the US Armed Forces, South Koreans, Australians, New Zealanders). The US mortuaries did not service the South Vietnamese, who had their own mortuaries. At the mortuary, the remains were washed and cleaned up before being fingerprinted. The remains also underwent a thorough dental examination, as well as being examined anatomically for known physical characteristics, such as scars and tattoos. Once these examinations were completed, the remains were then embalmed. All fingerprints were forwarded to Washington, DC for formal identity confirmation.

Once the remains had been identified and embalmed, they were wrapped in white gauze and placed into metal transfer cases for transportation back to the United States. The remains of our dead were flown to either Dover AFB in Delaware, or to Travis AFB in California, depending on which side of the Mississippi River their family lived on. The remains were then dressed in the proper dress uniform appropriate to their rank and service, and finally they were turned over to their families (and to civilian mortuaries) for burial.

Chapter 30

My 40 Round Magazine

In June 1967 I became distinctly aware that our enemy had some impressive weaponry. One of our patrols returned from inspecting the perimeter at Phu Bai with ten suspected Viet Cong prisoners. They also brought back an AK-47 rifle. It was the first AK that I had ever seen. It was a magnificent weapon, well made, with a beautiful wooden stock, and a 30-round magazine. I wish I had taken a picture of it.

My Dad was a machinist, I worked at a machine shop and I took shop classes in high school so I knew a little bit about metal working. We had a machine shop in the battery maintenance section. It was intended for repairing the guns, and to allow the motor transportation Marines to perform light mechanical repairs. Those guys couldn't perform a barrel change on an M53 or M55. All the heavy mechanical work was done by the maintenance unit based at Phu Bai airport. Our maintenance section could do a lot of repairs, stuff that the gun section could not do.

One day I took two 20-round magazines from an M-14 rifle over to the maintenance section. I cut the bottom off one magazine and cut the top off the other. I used an acetylene torch to weld the two magazine sections together. I then put two magazine springs into that monster, and I loaded it with forty rounds of 7.62mm full metal jacket ammunition. My thinking was to not take an M-14 with a forty-round magazine on patrol. I would use it defending the perimeter bunkers, and fighting holes that we had in the gun pits – or maybe even carry it on a rough rider when we were resupplying the gun detachments out on operations.

I asked Lieutenant Day if I could fire some test rounds to sight in an M14, but I didn't show him the magazine. He gave me permission. So, I went out to the edge of the perimeter wire and I fired off some rounds.

I don't want no teenage queen, I just want my M-14 … and my 40-round magazine. (This was a saying in boot camp in 1965.)

I shot off twenty-five or thirty rounds, but I couldn't fire all forty. The two springs would just not push up the remaining rounds. I added a third magazine spring, but then I found that I couldn't load forty rounds. I think the best I could manage was thirty-five rounds. When I test fired that M-14

Captured VC weaponry at the beginning of the Tet Offensive in February 1968. There are AK 47s as well as other types. The AK 47 was not the only fearsome weapon used by the communists. The weapons available to a VC platoon ranged from wartime French and German rifles, French submachineguns from the 1950s, captured ARVN weapons and rifles like the SKS and AK 47. (USMC)

with my magazine again, I had some problems with the rounds jamming in the magazine. There were other problems too. The M-14 was heavy and awkward, and the 40-round magazine was just too long. My 40-round magazine looked nice, but it never really worked right. I sure got some strange looks when I walked around the battery showing it off. I eventually cut it up and threw the scrap parts in a metal trash heap in the mechanic's workshop. It was a lesson learnt.

Note: A high school friend of mine saw this picture on the internet in 2016 when he tried ordering a 40-round magazine for another weapon of his. In 2021 another friend who lives in Florida also saw the picture and recognized the "jarhead", so I guess my picture has gone far and wide.

Chapter 31

Disciplining Marines

Whenever I had nothing else to do, I used to read about the Marine Corps' activities in "I" Corps on the battery's bulletin board. I always wanted to know what was going on in this war. There were postings on the bulletin board which described some of the misdeeds which had been perpetrated by a very small minority of our Marine brethren. There were Marines who were killing and raping civilians, and some who'd even killed other Marines. I found it really shocking to read that a Marine, who had had so much discipline drilled into him, could rape and murder civilians.

In the earlier years of the Vietnam War, Marine units had always taken care of their own minor disciplinary problems by assigning office hours, or time-honored punishment like filling sandbags. Some offenders were reduced in rank. A Marine could rise in rank quickly in Vietnam but could lose it just as fast. The punishments got more creative with time though. One unit had even dug a deep pit and put an offending Marine down in there with barbed wire around the top of the pit to prevent his escape. I had only seen pictures of that, and such measures had never been needed in the 1st Guns.

We had our own disciplinary issues however – and one Marine in particular who was a real problem. This Marine had somehow found a way to get past the guards on the outposts, to get through the wire perimeter and sneak out in the night to go to the closest village. He was caught for his offence when he came back into the perimeter in the wee morning hours, because he was drunk. While he slept off the booze, Lieutenant Day told me to watch him with my 45-caliber pistol. If the offender tried to get up and leave, I had orders to shoot him. When the drunk awoke and asked me what was going on, I told him that Lieutenant Day had ordered me to guard him, and that I'd shoot him if so much as left the tent. The man just laid back down. The MPs from headquarters came and got him, and he never came back to our battery.

On another occasion some of our senior NCOs turned an argument into a gun fight. I was walking over to the shower late one afternoon, and I heard a shot ring out. By instinct I just dropped to the ground. When I got up, I found to my astonishment that only 25 yards away from me a staff sergeant (E-6) and a gunnery sergeant (E-7) had got into an argument. The Gunny had pulled his M1911 Pistol and had shot the staff sergeant in the leg. Several other Marines picked the Staff up and put him in a Jeep, and they drove him over to A-Medical near the Phu Bai airport. We never saw the staff sergeant again. The gunnery sergeant (E-7) was reduced in rank to lance corporal (E-3). That's four stripes they took away from him. I never could get used to overseeing him on the fence working detail, because he was so much older than me.

Another Marine charged with guarding the perimeter front gate shot and killed a 10-year-old boy from the village. Many Marines had been buying marijuana from the villagers, and something had happened which caused the boy to steal the Marine's money. At least that's what the Marine said. This act made us no friends and we were on 100 per cent alert for a couple of days. The Marine was sent to the Da Nang Brig and eventually sent home to a jail to await his trial. After one year, they sent him back to Vietnam for a trial, but a Navy JAG got him off and all the charges were dropped. In the book *Trial By Fire* by Gary Solos, a marine JAG writes about the murders committed by Marines in Vietnam. It was a tough environment, which sometimes brought out the worst in people.

Chapter 32

Something is Wrong With Me

Towards the end of my tour I started to feel more tension. I often wondered what was wrong with me. I talked to our corpsman and asked him if I could go and see a psychiatrist. My little finger was shaking sometimes, I was increasingly nervous and I'd developed a sort of claustrophobia. I just did not feel right emotionally, and I felt like I was not going to get out of Vietnam alive.

"No, you do not want to go and see the psychiatrist" was his reply. He had just come from the Da Nang medical center and he'd seen the place where several nervous cases were being treated. "They will label you a nut case, something you do not want in your records." He got out a little bottle of medicine. "Take one of these pills when you feel agitated or nervous, but only one." He gave me a small brown plastic bottle containing a few Librium tablets.

The Librium pills actually seemed to help with the anxiety, but they also made me feel tired. Feeling tired was something I didn't like. I've always had a lot of energy and liked working or doing something to stay busy. I never liked just sitting around.

I also really had nobody to talk to in those weeks, because my best friend John Brophy was on another operation. I wondered if any of the others felt the same way that I did. Nobody ever talked about it if they did. Maybe it was just a short timer's feeling.

Chapter 33

Going on R&R

By the eleventh month of the tour, I was the corporal who did just about everything that a person could think of, and it had really made the time in Vietnam go by fast. Lieutenant Day asked me when I was going to go on R&R. I had been in Vietnam for almost twelve months and had never even had leave, so I replied "never."

Lieutenant Day told me that headquarters had opened up some leave opportunities in Hawaii, but that spaces were limited and they could only get the slots for Hawaii if they could fill a few leave slots in some of the other host countries. Several Marines were married and wanted to meet their wives in Hawaii. Lieutenant Day was one of them, and he convinced me to go anywhere but Hawaii.

Leave slots for Taiwan and Thailand were open, so I said "OK, I'll go to Thailand."

That opened one more slot for leave in Hawaii for him and the others. Now I didn't even know where Thailand was, but I thought maybe I needed a break from Vietnam. I hadn't spent much of my pay in Vietnam, and I really didn't want to spend the money either. I had heard it was very cheap living in Thailand, with an exchange rate of something like fourteen Thai baht to one American dollar. I had also heard that in Thailand they treated you like a king.

I dug out my summer uniform and dress shoes from the bottom of my sea-bag. It still had the Private First-Class strip on the sleeve. I hung up my uniform and it didn't look too bad for being in a sea-bag for almost twelve months. I shined my shoes and I was ready to go.

I got a ride to the Phu Bai airport, and I flew to Da Nang. Getting on a civilian airliner in Da Nang was nice. As we were flying, the captain asked if anybody wanted to come up into the cockpit and visit. I went forward. It was really a great view watching the clouds float by slowly. They were a very friendly crew, and they all thanked me for serving in Vietnam.

When the airplane landed in Thailand, we Marines went to an area to be briefed about the do's and don'ts in Thailand. We were encouraged to have a good time, but not to talk about Vietnam to anybody. I went to use the restroom and I saw a flush toilet for the first time in a whole year. I was just taken aback by that, something which had been so familiar was now so strange. I walked outside the airport into Thailand. I could not believe the bright colors around me. There were civilians wearing red, blue, yellow, and every other color you could think of. For twelve months all I had ever seen had been our green utilities, and white T-shirts, and the black pajamas of the Vietnamese. What a strange feeling I had seeing all those colors.

I met a cab driver, by the name of "Lucky". I told Lucky that I needed some civilian clothes. "No problem", Lucky said.

He took me to a tailor. I said I needed some dress slacks and a couple of shirts, and a belt. The tailors told me to strip down to my underwear and they gave me a rum and coke to drink. They took measurements and I watched them make the clothes as I drank the rum and coke. In minutes, I had pants, shirts, and a belt. Wow! I thought, what would be a great business to start in the USA someday.

I asked Lucky if he knew of a good hotel. "Of course," he said, and soon we headed out to the Hotel Rich. I got checked in and Lucky said to give your money to the hotel to keep it safe. I gave them my money. If I needed money, I just signed a ledger for what I took out. The hotel even had a swimming pool. It was my first time in a year to see a bed and bathtub. I must have soaked and slept the rest of the day away. Everywhere I went there were very nice and friendly people. Lucky wanted to show me the sites, and there were all kinds of places to go and see. There were river rides, Thai boxing matches, reptile farms, and all kinds of places to eat.

I met a few Marine Infantrymen who were also staying at the same hotel on R&R. I told them all about my nice cab driver, the new clothes, going out to eat and seeing some of the sites. They wanted to come with me. I asked Lucky and he said "yes, get in the car."

We piled in and he took us everywhere. We also spent a lot of time at the pool, just a bunch of big kids having fun. We really didn't talk about Vietnam, but it was a very memorable time for all of us. Of course, Lucky

Me in my new clothes at the Rich Hotel in Thailand. June 1967.

got a percentage of the large sums of money we are all spending. He even took me over to meet his family, and I had lunch with them one day.

After seven days in Thailand, I returned to Vietnam and to my battery. To my surprise Lieutenant Day said I could go on R&R again, but I had

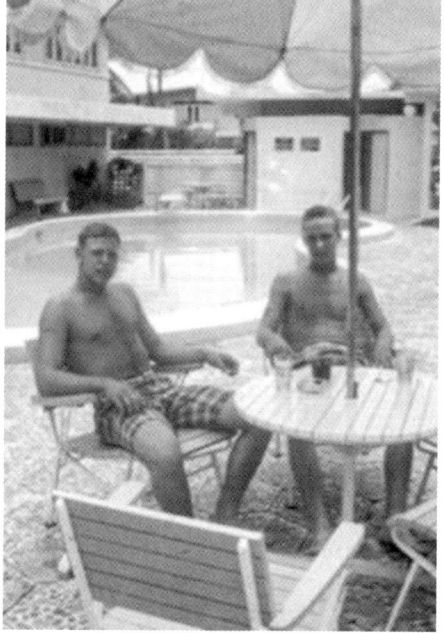

Above left: Bob Meyers and me.

Above right: Bob Meyer and me at the Rich Hotel's pool.

to go somewhere other than Hawaii. I happily took off for Thailand again for a second week of R&R. I went over to collect some of my pay for the trip and the sergeant clerk noticed I was a short-timer. He asked me where I wanted to go for my next duty station. I asked if there was anywhere besides California or North Carolina.

Another Marine had mentioned that he'd just come to Vietnam from Quantico, Virginia, and that the amount of liberty was great there. There were lots of pretty women in Virginia and it was close to the Nation's Capital. So, I selected Quantico – I had always wanted to see the Civil War battlefields.

I then made my way to the Phu Bai airport, flew on to Da Nang and there I met up with Bob Myers from my hometown. He and I had first met at the house of Marine recruiter Gunnery Sergeant Miller back in August 1965. Bob had joined the Marines a year after me.

Bob was serving in the 1st Amphibian Tractor Battalion (1st AMTRACKs) and he was going on R&R too. I asked a sergeant if Bob could go to Thailand instead of Taiwan, and he said yes. Bob and I had a great time visiting Thailand again and seeing all the sites. I found Lucky the cab driver again and he was surprised to see me. Now Lucky had two Marines to take care of.

After a fun visit to Thailand, I brought Bob back to the battery once we returned to Vietnam. When Lieutenant Day saw him, he asked, "who's this?" I told him Bob was from my hometown, and that I was wondering if he could stay for a few days with us at the battery. "Hilton, why do you do these things?" He asked.

Then he took Bob aside, asked him what outfit he was with, then made a radio call up to 1st Amtracks up on the Cua Viet river. He informed their commanding officer that Bob was staying for a few more days with 1st 155mm Guns in Phu Bai.

Despite those two weeks of R&R, being away from the gun battery in Thailand, and seeing my friend Bob Meyer, I still didn't feel much different. I really was a short timer. I had less than thirty days left in Vietnam. Someone even gave me a short timer's calendar. I hung it up on the wall in the hooch that the Seabees had built for us. Most of the time it was the gun crew that marked off the days for me. I just stayed busy, and those thirty days went by fast.

Bob with his shirt on with the gun crew cleaning the .50 Caliber machine gun up on the top of the bunker. I took Bob over to the Phu Bai airport a couple of days later.

Chapter 34

Injured Marines

An artillery battery was a very dangerous place to work, and many Marines got hurt during their service in the 1st Guns while I was in Vietnam.

Manhandling, lifting and dropping 100- and 200-pound artillery rounds and powder canisters, working on the heavy guns under sniper fire or mortar attack, the risks were high, and somebody was always getting hurt. Wounds like cut fingers, broken fingers and broken toes were common. On top of the hazards of working with ammunition, there was always someone who liked to play with fire and explosives.

Mike Adkinson hadn't been in our gun section for very long before he had a can of powder blow up in his face. Mike was putting powder in a fuse can and lighting it, then putting a rock in the fuse can. He wanted to see how far he could shoot that rock. Like a mortar. Boys will be boys.

When it didn't ignite, Mike removed the rock and looked down into the fuse can. It went up with a loud "BOOM".

I wasn't there to witness, but the crew said all that was left of his T-shirt was burning on his back. His face was burnt very badly and he was completely blind. A medevac came in and flew him to Da Nang. The gun crew packed up his sea-bag and everyone figured we would never see Mike Adkinson again.

A few weeks later I was just shocked to see Mike Adkinson walking into the gun section area carrying his sea-bag. His face looked like a very bad sunburn. I hugged him and I welcomed him back. We all asked: "what happened to you?"

He told us how the corpsmen had handed him over to medics, and they'd flown him to Da Nang. From there he was put on a flight to the Philippines, where they kept washing out his eyes. Eventually his sight came back.

He thought they were going to send him home. He was told: "No way Marine, you still have a lot of time to do in Vietnam."

Mike was never awarded a Purple Heart for those burns because his injury had not taken place during a fire mission.

All the hydraulic tubes are in the "well" of the gun (see picture) and they leak a lot. I was cleaning that area when a sniper started shooting at us. I stood up and reached for my rifle and caught my back on some of that metal in the well. It cut me badly, and the pain was so strong, I almost passed out. Probably saved my life, because it made me keep my head down. I never saw a Navy corpsman for stitches. No Purple Heart, but I still have a scar on my back.

One time I was walking along carrying a bucket of gasoline. A corpsman saw me heading over to a bunker with it and he just knew I'd end up spilling it. Sure enough, as I was climbing up the side of a bunker trying to hold the bucket steady, I slipped and fell and the gas splashed into my eyes. Anticipating this, the corpsman had grabbed a five gallon can of water and was already running towards me. "Open your eyes, Open your eyes!" he yelled. That corpsman poured all five gallons of water over my face. I was temporarily blinded, but the corpsman said my sight would come back.

Above left: Mike Adkinson holding a Claymore mine.

Above right: Bill Tindall broke his finger while closing one of the doors on the gun. (Courtesy of Ken Anderson)

Jerry Hunt (left) had shrapnel from a mortar round when the battery was getting mortared. He went to the corpsman and got several stitches and was bandaged up, but no Purple Heart. It's not even mentioned in his medical records. Ken Anderson (right) dropped one of the louver doors to the engine compartment on his hand and broke it.

This is the "well" of the gun, an area below the breech where the whole weapon can recoil when fired at high elevation.

It did, and I thanked the Lord. I just had the worst time with gasoline in Vietnam!

So many guys in the battery got hurt at one time or another. We had three corpsmen in the 1st 155mm Gun Battery, and they had to take care of eighty to a hundred Marines. We always had a corpsman go on operations when we detached a 155mm Gun and 8-inch howitzer from our battery to support larger operation. In fact we had an M53 and an M55 detached almost all the time. A second corpsman went on patrol daily with the Marines from the battery. Even today Marines still call their corpsmen "Doc".

It was so hot at Phu Bai that we often worked from 0600hrs until 1200hrs and then took from 1200 until 1500hrs off, unless we had a fire mission. After 1500hrs we'd start up and work until dusk. I was often on the perimeter fence detail, and it was especially hot out there in that white sand. During the break in the day, I stripped down to just my underwear and poured whatever remaining water I had with me in a five-gallon can over my head. A few minutes later, one of the Marines from the gun section came over and told me there was a water shortage because the Viet Cong had poisoned the well where we'd been getting our water. It would be a few days before we got any water delivered to us. I was glad that I had two canteens full of water – even if it was hot water by then.

(I shot an 8mm movie at this time. It's available on YouTube; search for: Phu Bai 1967 Larry Hilton)

Chapter 35

Last Patrol

Finally, July 1967 had arrived, and I knew I'd soon be going home. On the day of my last patrol of my tour, there were twelve of us Marines and one navy corpsman. Those were standard numbers for a squad size patrol. Sometimes we would exit the perimeter through the back gate. On that last patrol we went out the front gate. We turned right and walked down to the river, but we did not cross it. I was glad because I'd been getting ready to leave and go home. My rifle and my 782 web gear had been carefully cleaned. All of a sudden, we heard the loud rumble of thunder – but it was a clear day. One of the Marines pointed at the sky and told everyone to look up. We could see vapor trails high up in the blue sky, left by B-52 bombers. It was my first time to watch those big bombers drop their lethal payload so close to Phu Bai. It was a very strange feeling and sound.

We continued the patrol, walking a few miles around the Phu Bai area and then the patrol turned right again. Eventually we reached Highway 1. That paved road was easy to walk on, better than slogging through all that sand in the Phu Bai area. We walked south on the right side of the road. I noticed several civilians in the distance walking towards us on the same side, but off the road and on the sand.

We could see several of our tanks coming towards us, heading north. Each tank had several Marine riflemen piled on top of the engine decks. All of them were waving, and some shouted back and forth, just laughing, and joking, but I really could not hear what was being said. I was watching the civilians, like all of us should have been doing, but some of my patrol were distracted by the Marines on the tanks passing by.

After the tanks passed, I turned back around to continue walking. I almost tripped over a Vietnamese woman who came up behind me, exposed her private parts and started urinating right at my feet. She looked at me and started saying something in Vietnamese, but because she had been chewing that "Betel" that blackened her teeth, her mouth was all I could focus on (other than her urinating). I was in total shock. I looked at the Marine behind me and he was dumbfounded. That Vietnamese woman must have really gone out of her way to stop next to us, drop the pole and her two baskets, then pull up one black pajama pant leg to expose herself and urinate. Did that mean something? Just like when I'd arrived, I sensed these people did not want us here.

Vietnamese peasant women. (Courtesy of Seabee Ralph Yarbrough)

Chapter 36

Leaving the 1st 155mm Guns

On 11 July 1967, I awoke early in the morning, excited in the knowledge that I was leaving the 1st 155mm Gun Battery. It was hard to believe that I had been in this country for almost thirteen months to this day. I turned in my M-14 rifle, my 782-web gear, I ate my usual breakfast and then stood-to in morning formation. I saw the corpsman and he gave me more Librium to help keep me calm. "Remember, just take one if you need it," he said. It will be good for you to get home." I thanked him. I was just waiting for the engineers to clear the road outside our base camp and then I was going to get a ride over to the Phu Bai airport.

I knew that I was getting an early flight out of Phu Bai to Da Nang, and then flying out the next day to Okinawa. That's where my sea-bag was, stuff that I stored in that underground bunker thirteen months earlier. I made my way around the battery, saying my goodbyes and taking pictures with the last of my film in the couple of cameras that I had. Then I walked over to say goodbye to several guys in the motor transportation and maintenance sections. I saw Ken Marsh, and I wished him well.

I headed back over to the gun section where I gave away my jungle boots and my utilities. Also, I gave away my food tray, knife, fork and spoon, someone wanted my pillow and the small bookcase that I had made thirteen months earlier from some ammunition boxes. I was packed and ready to leave. I talked to Bill Tindall, and he told me he was glad that I was leaving – and how much he missed his parents. I just felt so bad for him. I told him to stay busy, with several months to go, it would make the time go faster. It's funny how you remember those things.

Ed Bowen was an artist, and he drew a very nice picture of a red 1957 Chevy. I used to tell stories to the gun crew about my red '57 Chevy that I'd raced around Covina and West Covina, back in California as a teenager. The picture was too big for me to carry inside my sea-bag, so I left it hanging on the wall next to the thirty-day calendar in the hooch. Leaving that behind was something I still regret to this day. I'm sure some North Vietnamese soldier now has that picture. He probably got it after the Marines left and the communists took over the country. It would be funny if it ever showed up in some North Vietnamese Museum. Ed Bowen had written "Hilton's Automotive" on the side of that red '57 Chevy.

Then there was trouble. "Hilton!" somebody yelled. "The first sergeant wants to see you."

Just when I thought I was going to get away with something, I didn't. I still had two weeks of extra guard duty to complete because I had failed an inspection. I had some rust on my rifle's trigger guard – a bad offence. The worst kind of offence for a Marine. I quickly went to see the first sergeant. He was standing outside his small hooch – and looked me straight in the eyes and said:

"Hilton! You thought that I didn't know that you're leaving? I could keep you here – you know that, don't you? Go on – Get out of here!"

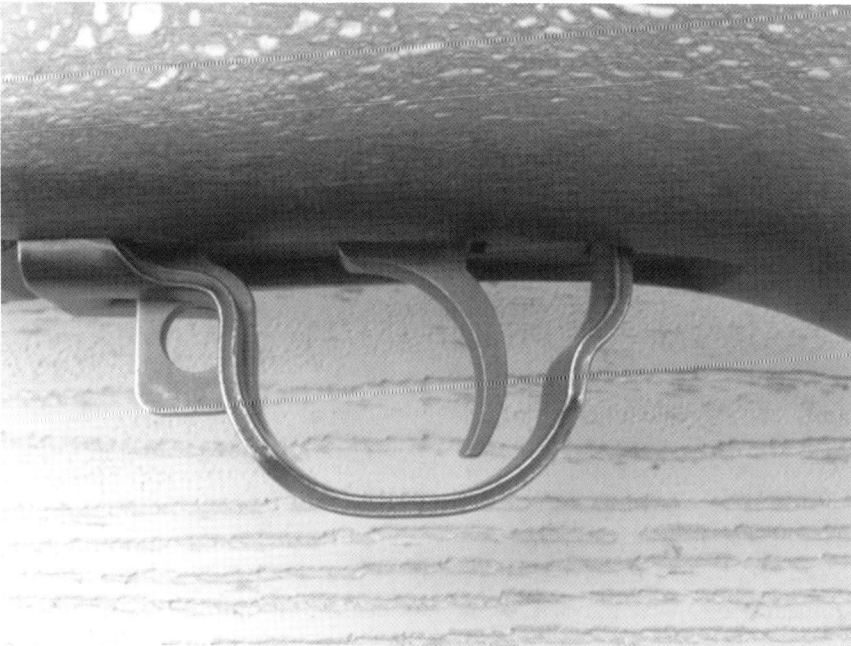

Rifle Trigger Guard…

I turned and ran – and that was the last time that I saw that first sergeant. I saw Glenn Kelly, the battery's clerk, and he told me he would drive me over to the Phu Bai airport. Kelly was one of the first Marines I'd met thirteen months earlier. He was on his first six-month extension – and would extend another six months. I caught the earliest flight out of Phu Bai.

1966-1966	Counteroffensive Phase II Campaign/Operation Hastings / Deckhouse II
1966-1966	Counteroffensive Campaign/Operation Orange
1966-1966	Counteroffensive Phase II Campaign/Operation Pawnee
1966-1966	Counteroffensive Phase II Campaign/Operation Pawnee II
1966-1966	Counteroffensive Phase II Campaign/Operation Macon
1966-1966	Counteroffensive Phase II Campaign/Operation Pawnee III
1966-1966	Counteroffensive Campaign/Operation Deckhouse I
1966-1966	Counteroffensive Phase II Campaign/Operation Deckhouse II
1966-1966	Counteroffensive Phase II Campaign/Operation Prairie
1966-1967	Counteroffensive Phase II Campaign/Operation Chinook I
1967-1967	Counteroffensive Phase II Campaign/Operation Chinook II

I would be credited for these Operations in the thirteen months that I spent in Vietnam.

Chapter 37

Da Nang

After landing in Da Nang, I headed over to a staging area, and there I saw some Marines who I had not seen in thirteen months. There were Marines that I had spent almost two months with at Camp Pendleton on mess duty and jungle training. I searched for and asked about Monte English, but nobody had seen him. Several of the guys remembered me getting chosen for placement in a 155mm gun battery all by myself on the first day when we all got assigned to our different outfits. From

I took this as we flew into Da Nang airport.

Tuesday, July 11, 1967

Above and left: Newspaper clip and a picture I took of the area where the B52 crashed when it finally stopped.

Wreckage of B52 at Da Nang

talking with the others, I finally found out that Monte English had been sent south to Chu Lai. I was surprised to find out that the Marines were operating that far south. I had always thought our area of operations only extended from Da Nang to the DMZ. A B-52 Bomber had crashed landed at the Da Nang airfield several days earlier, and several of the guys wanted to see that. I took a picture of the crash site and kept a newspaper clipping for posterity.

Later in the afternoon a bunch of us went over to the base club to get something to eat and drink. We naively left our sea-bags on some vacant racks in the staging area, trusting nobody would interfere with them. When I came back, I found that one of my cameras and my dress shoes had been stolen. It was an unwelcome return to the real world. The next morning, we got up early, ate and then headed over to the airfield. There was a commercial jet waiting for us, and we loaded aboard right from the tarmac – assisted by very friendly stewardesses in short skirts. They had us all seated in the Boeing 707 jet in just a few minutes, and then handed everyone a coke to drink while we waited to take off.

No group of newbie Marines were coming in from Okinawa as we veterans ending our tour departed; no visible change from what I'd experienced in June 1966. Eventually the incoming Marines would just fly from the United States directly to Da Nang, on a commercial aircraft and fly back directly to El Toro Marine base. Often they just cut the stop in Okinawa out entirely. I was seated between two Marines I didn't know, but I wasn't planning to talk very much because I had pulled out my Librium. As I opened the plastic container, the guy on my left asked me what I was taking. I told him my corpsman had given me some medicine to keep me calm. He asked if he could have one, and then the Marine on the right held out his hand. I gave them both one pill. I just wondered if there were more people on that plane who felt the same way that I did.

Finally, we felt the airplane move as it began taxiing to the runway. As that big 707 lifted off everyone on board began to yell with excitement. It was just too hard to believe that thirteen months in Vietnam was finally over. I just sat back while the jet climbed high above the warzone that was Vietnam. I thought about home after having been away from home for such a long time, the 1st 155mm Gun Battery, the gun crew, those men who'd been killed – and that Vietnamese woman urinating. I slowly drifted off to sleep. Four hours later the three of us had to be awakened in our seats on the runway in Okinawa. One of the Marines asked me "what was in that pill you gave us?"

We collected our sea-bags and we checked into the staging area, and we were searched for weapons. The wall inside the staging area was loaded with just about everything you can imagine. There were rifles, pistols, hand grenades, belts of machine gun ammunition, bayonets, and Marine Ka-bar knives. Young Marines were thinking they could sneak these weapons and ammunition home as souvenirs all the time.

We marched over to temporary quarters in some empty barracks, and then about thirty of us went over to the underground bunkers to get the same uniforms that we had left there thirteen months earlier. We had to scrape away the weeds and dirt around the big steel front door of that bunker before we could open it. Sure enough, just as we had left them, one hundred sea-bags were stacked neatly up. They called out our names written on the sea-bags. Thirty of us took ours and left, and they closed the door. They said the others would come in the next few days to collect theirs.

Back at the barracks, there were women walking up and down the showers calling out the different Marines' names. It seemed strange that these women were oblivious to the sight of the naked Marines showering as they were yelling out their names to let them know their uniforms were ready. The guys in the showers had given their uniforms to these women to sew new stripes on them. They even had sewing machines set up in the barracks. One lady even ironed one of the summer uniforms for me to wear going home. It sounded like a great idea, because I was a PFC when I went to Vietnam but now, I was a corporal. I gave my uniforms to one of the women and told her I was going to take a shower.

On the next day while I was getting ready to go into the mess hall, the Marine in front of me turned and told me that enemy rockets and mortars had hit Da Nang airfield. There had been lots of casualties and the airport was closed. We had just made it out of there.

A newsreel report of the attack on Da Nang airfield is available to view on YouTube, just search: "Viet Cong rocket attack on U.S. Da Nang Airbase in Vietnam HD".

The mess hall was crowded with Marines coming and going. I saw a Marine sitting alone at a table and I sat across from him. He asked me if I was in the hospital. I said no, I had just arrived yesterday from Vietnam. He said that only patients ate at this table, so I asked what was wrong with him. He said the medics had been draining liquid off his brain, and turned his head, and I could see where his head was shaved to the scalp, and he had a bandage on it. I asked why they were doing that and he told me that while in Vietnam he had started to feel nervous and his hand was shaking, so he went to the hospital in Da Nang and they'd sent him to Okinawa.

I immediately recalled my corpsman warning not to go to Da Nang to see a psychiatrist. I told him my corpsman had given me Librium and showed him the pills. I said, "I just take one pill if I start feeling nervous."

I opened the small container and I showed him the black and light blue capsules. I also said, "maybe you just need to go home and get around family and friends."

I still wondered how many of us Marines felt this way.

The truth was I still felt nervous. I spent the rest of the evening at the club. I listened to a lot of war stories, but it really didn't make me feel any better. Marines who'd served with units from Da Nang all the way north to the DMZ had something to say about that war. They had come from infantry and artillery; there were clerks, cooks and truck drivers. It seemed that everyone had heard our 155mm guns firing at different times. Those things were loud and unpopular.

One Marine was carrying an old French bolt-action rifle. He told me he'd killed a Viet Cong sniper and they'd let him keep the rifle as a souvenir. I asked him what his next duty station was, and he replied "A drill instructor at the Recruit Depot in San Diego, California." He said it was the last thing he wanted to do.

Most of the guys were going to Camp Pendleton in Southern California, and several were headed to the East Coast to the 2nd Marine Division. Nobody had heard of Quantico, Virginia, and until recently neither had I. After blowing off steam at the club for several hours, we all headed back to barracks and went to bed. All I could think about was that poor Marine in the mess hall and that rocket attack on the Da Nang airfield. We had just missed that attack by one day.

Early the next morning we all lined up to get on the commercial jet back to the USA, but we received a small needle prick in the left forearm in the line. We were told that we would be examined when we got to El Toro Marine Base in Southern California, just to see if we had any reaction. The corpsman said the spot would be infected if any of us did have something. Our first stop was at Nome, Alaska, to refuel. It was the middle of July and too cold to get off and walk around. I went to the opened door and felt the cold air and saw an Air Force ground crewman in a heavy jacket.

We continued the flight to El Toro Marine base. When I got off that plane, I was checked but I hadn't any reaction to the needle prick in my arm. We were ordered to check in and to pick up our orders and pay. Several among us did have reactions – I could see the infected area on their arms. Those guys had to go see a corpsman, but I never heard what they'd caught. Who knows what kind of a disease's one could catch in Vietnam?

Chapter 38

Welcome Home

On 15 July 1967, I found myself standing in front of the Greyhound Bus station in West Covina, California – waiting for my parents to pick me up. Just a couple of days earlier I had been standing in the morning formation with eighty other Marines in South Vietnam. I'd survived thirteen months with the 3rd Marine Division. I'd left Marine Air Station El Toro on 15 June 1966 and had arrived back at El Toro that very morning at 0600 hours, thirteen months later, to the day. I was given a bunch of money, the orders to my next duty station, and thirty days' leave. Just that fast, I was processed out.

I flagged down the first cab that I saw and headed for the closest Greyhound bus station. I was in West Covina by 1030 hrs. As I stood there in my hometown, I do not think I have the words to describe the feelings I had. People offered to drive me home. I thanked them and said that my parents were coming. The bus station was busy, and several people were standing outside as a bus pulled up to unload and load passengers.

I had missed my family, friends, and neighbors. The only contact I had with them was letter writing. Just then my parents pulled up in our car and kind of blocked in the bus (and the car was partially sticking out into the street). My parents jumped out of their car. I had never seen my Dad move that fast. As soon as I saw them, I started to cry. My Mom was crying, and my Dad had tears in his eyes as he hugged and held me. Right out in front of all those people we were crying with joy and we hugged one another. I looked up, and the bus driver and passengers were wiping their eyes too. I was home!

Now that I was home, let the party begin! For the next two days at least thirty people came over to our house to see me. I received a great welcome home, and many thank you cards. People gave me money to go out to dinner, and lots of hugs, kisses, and handshakes. It was a great neighborhood to grow up in and to return to. Naturally, we all drank a lot of "Brew 102" beer that weekend (you could buy a six pack of that beer for $1.02…).

My tour in Vietnam had passed while most of the American public still supported the war. The protests and turning against soldiers hadn't happened yet. That all changed really fast. Within a few months, Marines returning from Vietnam to El Toro would be advised to change into civilian clothes, before going to the airport or the bus stations, to avoid possible harassment.

A woman asked me some time later; "What did you take from your Vietnam experience?" I answered, "a closeness to our Lord."

Another woman asked: "Do you thank Him?"

"Often…" was my reply.

Over 3,000 US Marines were killed in Vietnam during my thirteen-month tour.

END PICTURES

Top: Family and friends celebrated in our backyard. Leroy, bottom right, my youngest brother.

Above left: Me and my mom and dad.

Above center: Covina High School classmate Mike Varley (CHS-65. in the National Guard. Larry Hilton Marines (CHS-65) Don Caouette (CHS-63) still in the Marines. 1960 Chevrolet Impala in the background.

Above right: Dick Jones (CHS-65) In the Air Force, Ron Hilton, my older brother (CHS-62) just out of the Army, and Steve Kline (CHS-67), who would join the Army in a few years.

Epilogue

My high school friend Allen Jagielo, who'd told me about the Marines landing in Vietnam in March 1965, did join the Army. He was killed in October 1967 as an Army Medic with the 28th Infantry (Black Lions). His Company was in the lead of an advance, when they walked into an ambush.

Above left: Allen Jagielo, Covina High School 1965.

Above right: GY SGT Gary L. Sloan was my senior drill instructor, and I found his grave marker years later. Sergeant Thompson and Corporal Zavala could not be found.

Above left: Mike Varley, my first childhood friend who I'd met in West Covina back in December 1953 had gone into the Army National Guard during the Vietnam war – serving as a machine gunner. He stayed in the Guard for six years. He also was home when I arrived home from Vietnam in July 1967. It was great to see him and all the others that came by to welcome me home. We text and talk often.

Above right: Roy Bell with his dog in Vietnam.

Sixty US soldiers were killed and another sixty-eight were wounded in about three minutes. The book *They Marched into Sun Light* by David Maraniss tells the whole story – and it's worth reading.

Don Caouette, whom I joined the Marines with, was my friend since 1953. He was wounded in Vietnam by machine-gun fire and was sent to the Philippines to recover. Don only had a two-year enlistment and separated from the Marines in 1967. Don passed away young at the age of 45 because of heart problems.

Brad Begin, a high school friend that joined the Marines with me, was sent to Vietnam, but their plane landed in Japan to refuel, they were asked if anyone had an MOS for a supply clerk. Brad was the only one that raised his hand, so he was taken off the plane – and he stayed in Japan until he

Roy Bell, my childhood friend whom I'd met in 1954, joined the US Air Force and went to Vietnam. He was a Crew Chief on a Caribou airplane. He and I wrote to each other while both of us were in Vietnam in 1967. One of his jobs was picking up the remains of soldiers from collection points all over Vietnam and taking them back to the mortuary in Saigon. Roy and I visited and talked up until he passed in December 2016. I am still in touch with his daughter Tracy.

Donald Caouette receiving his Purple Heart.

Above and right: Don Caouette's grave and seen with his family.

separated from the Marines. I would try to see him when I came home to visit my parents. Brad passed away on 26 January, 2019.

Monte English's name wasn't on the Vietnam wall when it opened in 1982. I had tried to find him for years, but I just never could. I did see a picture of Monte on Facebook in 2010. When I tried to contact him, I received a call from Monte's oldest son and daughter. His daughter and I talked for hours. Monte had passed away from pancreatic cancer in 2010; he was just 62 years old.

Right: Monte English

Below: Monte's grave

Tom Janeway – the Marine I was in artillery school with – and I drove across the country from California to Camp LeJeune in January 1966, and went to Vietnam on "Old Shaky". I saw him once in Vietnam. I found him on Facebook and his wife contacted me to say that Tom didn't remember me – until I sent him this picture. This was one of the trucks I drove.

Glenn Kelly and I became close friends after he left our 155mm gun section, and he became the battery's clerk. Kelly extended his tour two times, and he spent twenty-five months in Vietnam. I looked for him for years but could never find him. I found Glenn's wife on Facebook in 2018 and she told me he'd died in 2012 from various cancers, all Agent Orange related. He had been receiving 100 per cent disability from the VA.

John Brophy and I had became corporals (E-4) at the same time in Vietnam. We'd only been in the Marines fourteen months, and we were both 19 years old. My wife Susan, our youngest daughter Kasey, and I visited John and his family in Lake Erie, Pennsylvania, in 1986 and stayed the weekend. We are still friends to this day.

Above left: John had left the Marines in 1969, but then he joined the Army's National Guard (and stayed in for twenty-five years). John was an E-7 when he left the Army. He visited me once in Virginia while he was doing his two weeks of duty at Fort A.P. Hill (renamed Fort Walker), just outside of Fredericksburg, Virginia.

Above right: Ken Marsh on the steps of 155mm Gun number three was promoted to corporal at the age of 19.

Me (left) and Ken Marsh in 2016 at my home in Fredericksburg, Virginia. Ken extended for six months in Vietnam and made sergeant. He was sent to Camp LeJeune, North Carolina and sent on a Mediterranean cruise. He would have been promoted to staff sergeant (E-6) but he separated from the Marines. He didn't want to go back to Vietnam.

Leland Caskey (left) from Nebraska was 28 years old and was drafted into the Marines. Everyone called him the old man. He told me that his wife wrote to him every day for thirteen months. In this picture Leland and I are getting ready to go on patrol. We have visited each other in Nebraska and in Virginia.

189

One day I got on the internet and just typed in Willis Penfold, another friend from Vietnam. I'm thinking there couldn't be too many guys named Willis Penfold in Michigan. One name came up and he seemed to be the right age. I called the number, and sure enough, it was the same Marine that came into our battery back in October 1966. He said "Larry you are not going to believe this, but I'm sitting here at my desk looking at a picture of you." He had found the photo recently, and it was sitting out on his desktop. We have been talking and mailing pictures for years.

Willis Penfold (right) and another Marine getting water for the shower tank and washing Jeeps and trucks. It's no wonder we all have Agent Orange related problems. That river must have been full of Agent Orange. (Willis Penfold)

Battery at Gia Le in 1966. (Courtesy of Bob Simington)

The Communist Army base in 2015 when Bob Simington visited it. They would not let him in. (Courtesy of Bob Simington)

Bob is the second from the left. This is his crew of FDC Marines leaning against the FDC bunker at Phu Bai. (Courtesy of Bob Simington)

Bob Simington memorized the location of our battery in Phu Bai, and he located exactly where it was with a GPS in 2017. The Vietnamese had run a highway right through the middle of where the FDC bunker was once located. (Courtesy of Bob Simington)

This was an easy crew of Marines to be with. I cannot remember any of them complaining if told to go and do something. Jerry Hunt was from La Grange, Kentucky. He passed away from Agent Orange related sicknesses on 5 July 2021. He'd come into an existing gun section, and he fit right in when he arrived in the 1st 155mm Guns in February 1967. Jerry never complained and always volunteered to go help others that were under attack. He was wounded by shrapnel but never received a Purple Heart. Jerry gave his camera to someone, and had him take this picture of our gun crew. None of us can remember who that photographer was. Jerry and I had been talking and texting for eighteen months before his passing. Jerry was a good Marine – Rest In Peace my friend.

Left to right: Ken Anderson and Ed Bowen. Some of the best Artillerymen that I served with.

Above: Ken Anderson (left) and Ed Bowen at the Marine Corps National Museum March 2018.

Left: Ken Anderson was blown out of a 5-Ton truck that he was driving when he ran over a landmine. He landed in a rice paddy full of water. His first thoughts were to get his M-14 rifle, which was still in the truck that was on fire. Several Marine infantrymen came to his aid. The patches on his coat sleeve pretty much say it all for this Marine Cannoneer. Ken and I talk often.

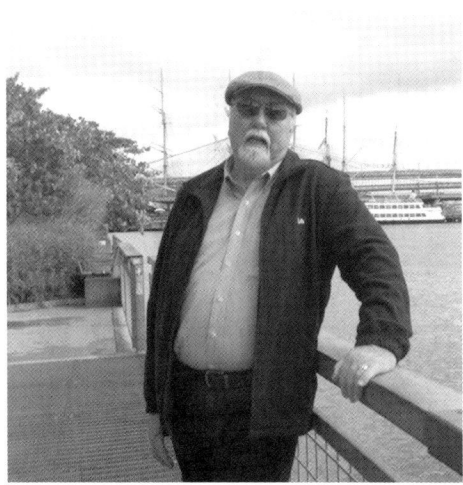

Above left: Joseph V. Pulsinelli, 72, passed away on 5 April 2018. He served his country proudly in the US Marine Corps.

Above right: When Bill Tindall arrived in Vietnam, he and several other Marines were sent out to an abandoned mortar battery to guard overnight. They didn't want the Viet Cong to take it over. "All you need," he was told, "is your helmet, flak jacket, and rifle."

They were there for thirty days. Bill said it was not an enjoyable time. Bill and I have talked and texted on and off for a couple of years. He and his wife are living in Northern California.

Earl Bradish and I have been in contact since 2020. He sent me this picture. He left the Marines and joined the US Air Force and was even in Special Forces. I would love to hear some of his stories.

Left: Ernie Gutierrez, who was killed at PK-17, thanked me once when I was carrying 200-pound HE rounds to him during a Fire Mission. It's strange how I remember him thanking me. His nephew wasn't born at the time, but we have emailed each other some.

Below: Michael Himmerick, our corpsman who was killed at PK-17. Some of Michael's family have contacted me. His nieces never knew him, because they were not born yet, and they have asked about their uncle. We emailed some, and their mother, Michael's sister, was interested too. I sent them the After-Action Report from the Marine Corps records from the attack where Michael was killed.

REMEMBERED

Michael is honored on the Vietnam Veteran's Memorial in Washington DC. Name inscribed at VVM Wall, Panel 17e, Line 111.

COMMENDATIONS

★ Purple Heart
★ Combat Action Ribbon
★ National Defense Service Medal
★ Vietnam Campaign Medal
★ Vietnam Service Medal
★ Navy Presidential Unit Citation
★ Vietnam Gallantry Cross
★ Navy Good Conduct Medal
★ Navy Expeditionary Medal

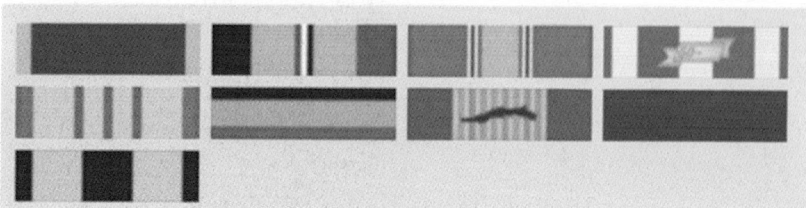

Remembering a few Veterans. (L–R) Dick Jones (USAF), Ron Hilton my brother (US ARMY), Steve Kline (US ARMY), Larry Hilton (USMC). All from West Covina but went to Covina High School. Steve Kline Passed away from lung cancer in 1996. This picture was taken in July 1967 at the Hilton family home on Shamwood Street West Covina.

Eight alumni from Covina High School would be killed in Vietnam. Donald W. Evans Jr. was awarded the Medal Of Honor posthumously by President Johnson in 1967.

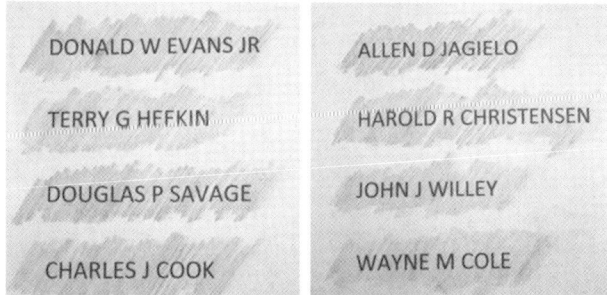

DONALD W EVANS JR

ALLEN D JAGIELO

TERRY G HEFKIN

HAROLD R CHRISTENSEN

DOUGLAS P SAVAGE

JOHN J WILLEY

CHARLES J COOK

WAYNE M COLE

The author today.

Appendix

(By M.P. Robinson)
Photos from USMC Operations in 1966–7

The period between mid-1966 and mid-1967 was an incredibly hard time for the 1st and 3rd Marine Divisions in I Corps, the northernmost part of the Republic of Vietnam (RVN). Indeed, during the spring of 1967, the intensity of the operations and the limited resources available to the III Marine Amphibious Force caused the US Army theater commander, General Westmoreland, to rethink how I Corps was to be adequately defended. At the same time, the North Vietnamese Army began its protracted campaign of infiltration through the demilitarized zone (DMZ) along the northern border and through the Laos border in the northwest part of the RVN. While the US Army assembled Task Force Oregon to reinforce the areas south of Chu Lai with Army brigades borrowed from the divisions further south, the two Marine divisions shifted north. This move culminated in the creation of the US Army's 23rd Infantry Division in the summer of 1967.

The 3rd Marine Division, to which the 1st 155mm Gun Battery was assigned, was tasked with taking over the border area. The 1st 155mm Gun Battery's role in this time was frequently long-range artillery fire missions in support of units moving northwards to the DMZ or fighting in the contested border zone. The battery was frequently employed to hit targets identified by Marine reconnaissance patrols and could be called upon to fire in general support of the four artillery battalions of the 12th Marine Regiment. The collection of Marine Corps photos seen here document some of the operations which took place while Larry Hilton was serving in Vietnam.

Taken on 19 July 1966, this photo shows a CH46A Sea Knight from the 1st Marine Air Wing's HMM-265 lifting a 105mm howitzer to new positions in support of the 3rd Marine Division during Operation Hastings. Operation Hastings was planned to use the 3rd Marine Division to occupy the northern border. The USMC conducted seventy-six large operations with its 1st and 3rd Marine Divisions in the coastal plain which ran all the way up through I Corps between August 1966 and July 1967, and focused an increasingly large portion of the 3rd Marine Division onto operations in the demilitarized zone (DMZ) between the border of North Vietnam and the Republic of Vietnam during Larry Hilton's tour. All of these operations required artillery support from the USMC's artillery battalions.

An M53 with its crew in Vietnam. The 1st 155mm Gun Battery, was equipped in peacetime with six Guns, 155mm, Self-Propelled M53, but early during the "1st Guns" deployment to Vietnam three M53s were exchanged for Howitzers, 8-inch, Self-Propelled M55. This was accomplished in order to balance the firepower available to each of the Fleet Marine Force (FMF) batteries deployed to support the III Marine Amphibious Force.

A Marine mans an M2 HB .50 Browning heavy machine gun during Operation Onslow in October 1967. The weapon is mounted on an M76 Otter, an all terrain tracked transport vehicle. (USMC)

A US Army Caribou transport, seen here in 1964 during the MACV advisory period. The USMC operated a medium helicopter squadron from Da Nang in the same period to support the ARVN. (US NARA)

A stream crossing in I Corps by three Marines in 1966. The nearest man is armed with an M3A1 "Grease Gun", a Second World War era .45 caliber submachine gun used for many years as a weapon for drivers and vehicle crews. The Marines brought many older weapons along to Vietnam in 1965 because they were available, reliable and familiar. (USMC)

Marines examining AKMs and an M1 Carbine captured from a Vietcong hide in early 1968. (USMC)

Marine infantrymen moving through swampy terrain during Operation Chinook II in 1967. These Marines are carrying M14 rifles and wearing flak vests over full webbing.

Marines firing with new M16s in 1967. The M16 had many skeptics amongst the Marines who had been trained on the M14. The M16 had many teething troubles during its first months in Vietnam, some of which were related to cleaning procedures, others to minor design changes, and of which were caused by defective ammunition. (USMC)

Marines marching through the hamlet of Gia Do in March 1967. No matter the type of unit, Marine tactics included daily patrolling in order to assure perimeter defense as well as to demonstrate their presence to the locals. In artillery units which were already under strength to begin with, this was an additional burden which wore men thin.

In March 1967, in the vicinity of Gia Do, Marines come into contact with Viet Cong or North Vietnamese Army during a patrol. In an instance such as this, the platoon radio man was absolutely vital in calling in fire from the nearest artillery unit. This would permit the patrol to break contact with any luck, and if combat air patrol was available, air support could be called in within a matter of minutes.

If tube artillery could not immediately support a platoon in trouble, the Marine infantry battalions included 60mm mortar sections, short-range weapons which could be carried by a team of three men.

The M72 Light Anti Tank Weapon (LAW) was a 66mm disposable rocket launcher which supplemented and then replaced the M20 3.5 inch bazooka in Army and Marine units in Vietnam. Designed to destroy tanks, in Vietnam it was used to take out enemy bunkers. (USMC)

Representative of the Rough Rider convoys of Larry's days in Vietnam are these armed trucks on Highway 6 near Da Nang. This photo was taken some months after Larry returned to the USA and belonged to the 7th Motor Transport Battalion, USMC in 1968.

A lieutenant from the 3rd Marine Division's 3/4th Marines following the capture of Hill 484 in September 1966 during Operation Prairie. Hill 484 sat in close proximity to the DMZ and was considered an important tactical position in controlling the surrounding area. He is armed with an M1 carbine, a weapon popular with Allied as well as enemy forces (who had captured substantial stocks of this weapon from the French and from the ARVN).

Men of the 3/4th Marines in combat near the DMZ on 30 September 1966. The Marine in the background is presumably carrying a 3.5 inch rocket forward to a nearby bazooka team.

Cannon cockers of the 12th Marines in action supporting Operation Prairie with 105mm howitzer fire in October 1966. The 1st Guns' 155mm M53 Self-Propelled Guns were frequently used to augment the firepower of field artillery units from the four battalions comprising the 12th Marine Regiment. The move up to the DMZ resulted in all units of the 3rd and 1st Marine Divisions being spread very thinly across the eastern coastal plain of I Corps and across the northern border along Highway 9 east to Khe Sanh.

One of the standard weapons issued to Marine units in Vietnam was the 40mm M79 grenade launcher, seen here being fired in 1967 in Vietnam, unit unknown.

Navy Corpsmen taking cover from enemy fire during Operation Chinook II in 1967.

Marines under fire running across a bridge during Operation Chinook II. The early operations against the NVA produced very high casualties in Marine units, in part because the enemy was equipped with conventional artillery firing across the DMZ.

Above: A Marine fire team from the 3rd Marine Division during Operation Chinook II. The heavily laden machine gun team is engaging enemy positions with a tripod mounted M60, employed for sustained fire.

Left: A Marine from the 3/4th Marines with his new M16 in May 1967 during Operation Chinook.

The M20 and M20A1 Bazookas were employed by the USMC in Vietnam by all Marine rifle battalions. Lightweight, simple and reusable, the main thing to remember was to respect the weapon's powerful backblast. (USMC)